The Body Talks
and I Can Hear It

As Jeanies' ex-husband and for-ever friend, I am truly grateful for the personal and spiritual transformation she guided me through, helping me to clear recent and ancient issues I had stored away, which were affecting my life and personal relationships.

Jeanie has a gift she was sent to share, through her work and through this book: to help us learn about our physical, mental, and emotional selves, how we store our issues and problems in our body, and how to become more aware of our body when it speaks to us. Our body holds our answers. She is helping us learn to listen to our Selves, and thereby more fully BE who we are. –Rich Juarez, San Diego, CA

Jeanie helps you understand what's true for your soul and spirit in order to live, not just exist. –Jan Walker, Dallas, TX

Jeanie's insight and love have filled my heart and lightened my spirit. –Linda Patrick, Silver Spring, MD

You helped me find my Self, that other space of who I am, and that means so much to me, because it's helped me through this dis-ease (AIDS). You've helped me go on that road to my greater Self. –Jimmy Lisenbee, Dallas, TX

The universe has blessed us with unconditional love, support, and encouragement through Jeanie—a gift few of us have ever received, but all deserve. –*With Love*, Theresa M. Geimer, Reiki Master, Columbia, MD

As one fortunate enough to have done some individual work with Jeanie, I highly recommend this work and book as an interpretive guide for those on an inward journey of self-discovery and unfoldment. This work is essential reading for those who want to recognize and maximize the opportunities that lie ahead in the next millennium.

–Debbie Miller, Long Beach, CA

Jeanie Lemaire has been my friend and mentor for the past eight years. I could write a book myself about how she helped me transform my life. Thanks for believing in me, Jeanie.

–Janet Pittrich, Carlsbad, CA

Those who know Jeanie, know–and those of you who don't, have a friend you haven't met–for she is someone who can penetrate the barriers and the boundaries, and the truth is, you have company you haven't yet met. It's gentle and it's good–wake up!

–With Love, Tom White, La Verne, CA

Jeanie Lemaire is a magnificent Being. Through her heart and hands she facilitates us to allow ourselves to connect with our oneness.

–Rebecca Schroedter-Ion, Los Osos, CA

In working four years with Jeanie, she has shown me the way to believe in the magic of life . . . and to have the courage to live in the way that is truthful to me. What a true blessing she is, and her teachings have been. When we met, she shared with me, in her humorous way, that I appeared to have been 'run over by a Mack truck' in life, and she has shown me how to get out of the way of judgment and experience daily my own contributions to life. I don't believe I would still be here if I hadn't met and worked with Jeanie. I am truly honored to know her.

–Patty Conte, Los Angeles, CA

The Body Talks
and I Can Hear It

by

JEANIE LEMAIRE

Balancing
Arts

ISBN# 0-9648540-0-7

Library of Congress Catalog Card Number: 95-80304

Published by Balancing Arts
P.O. Box 3864, La Habra, CA 90632-3864
Telephone (310) 694-1229

♡ The cover art was brought into heartfelt created form by Rachel Harwell.
♡ The thoughts of Brock Tully from the series, *Reflections for Someone Special* (Brock Tully Press, 1983: Distributed in U.S. by Hay House Inc., 1-800-654-5126) are included herein with permission of the author.

Printed in the United States of America

10   9   8   7   6   5   4   3   2   1

Dedication

This book is lovingly dedicated to

YOU,

the Being who lives inside your Physical form,

as your "Self"—

an Incredible,

Magnificent,

Priceless

GIFT—

which you are,

always have been,

and always will be . . .

♡

♡ ♡ ♡

No matter where I wander,
no matter where I roam—
I play my part with a happy heart,
The whole wide world's my home.

—from "The Oneness Space"

♡ ♡ ♡

♡ TABLE OF CONTENTS ♡

♡ PREFACE ♡

Have you ever stopped to wonder how a person gets around to writing a book? My thought was that someone must wake up one morning and say, "Gee, I think I'll write a book." And then, of course, the person goes and makes an outline, gathers information, presents it to a publisher, and *voilà!*—the book appears on a bookshelf in some bookstore.

However, as I discovered one morning, there is another way that books get written. I was talking over the phone with a very special man in my life about some of the work that I do. My background is in massage therapy, and for years I have been doing what I call Integrated Body Therapy and Personal Growth Facilitation. Translated, this means I consult with the body, or have the three densest bodies—the Physical, Mental and Emotional—speak to me. I do my work with my eyes closed, enabling me to be fully "in touch" with someone. Over the years, more and more information has been brought forth via the "Being" that resides inside each of these, our human bodies. After sharing this and more with my friend, he asked, "Have you ever thought about writing a book on this?"

And I, of course, replied as anyone would, "Isn't there already a book, if not several, on the subject?"

He responded, "I haven't seen any, and you know I look extensively for topics like this in the bookstore. Have you?"

And I thought and thought some more. "Let's see, there are charts for reflexology and plenty of information on the nine physical body systems, even books on nerves, muscles, and bones." But the fact was that I hadn't actually seen anything in print that referred to the integration of the three natures, through which we, the Being, express our Self. As I shared this data with clients and other therapists, I began to realize that much of this perception is not presently expressed in print.

So now I see another way that books get written: they literally well up inside and finally overflow onto paper as certain information and awareness builds up and cries out to be available to others. With this in mind, I began an active search for any and all books related to my work. What few I found were dry and lacking an essential ingredient—humor. As an ordained Spiritual Advisor and Healer, I decided right then to write this book from the standpoint of my new ministry, which is called F.U.N. All you have to do to join this ministry is to have a little FUN each week, and by the way there are no restrictions stating that you can't have a LOT of FUN each week. Minimum membership, however, is at least one moment when, unexpected by you, totally unplanned and free flowing, you experience total abandonment—and thereby lighten your load by some amount, no matter how incremental. (I've discovered that the base definition of *enlightenment* is simply "to lighten up," and to me that seems to suggest not taking things *quite* so seriously.) To keep up with the fast-growing membership of the ministry of F.U.N., identification cards are not issued—both to save the trees and to delete paperwork—but each member knows that their participation and contribution to the ministry is strengthened each and every time they brighten their day with some good old-fashioned FUN.

So, I am going to ask you to let go of any notion or expectation you might have as to the value of this book in your life and to let your inner eyes do the walking through this three-way mirror to the Self that you are about to experience. And, as I constantly remind my clients, please take what you like, but don't litter. Just throw the remaining notions—that is, any that don't suit you—in the garbage. After all, each and every one of us is an

Incredible, Magnificent, Priceless Gift, just by being here in form on the planet, and no matter if we do life right, wrong, upside down, inside out, backwards, or topsy-turvy, the gift is in our presence here—our personal worth is a given.

You see, whether or not you gravitate to this book is not my concern, since none of us has the final say in the development of another, anyway—only of ourselves. Sometimes the hardest thing in the world for any of us to do is to let go of something or someone we love, enough for them to grow within themselves. We tend to want others to come with us on our journey, because we are filled with the wonder of discovery and the excitement of new awareness. However, it usually causes both parties great pain when we attempt to *force* another to move to a level that is greater than their current awareness. Besides, even if we could force them to do as we do, they wouldn't get to learn their lessons in their own way, and that is a crime. So the best that any of us can hope to be is as a Living Example for each other, by being our fullest Self.

In short, if you are currently determined to remain separate from the connected whole, to continue to be what has been perceived as "normal" (going along with unconscious habit energy, or as dictated by sources outside your true Self), this book will be of little use to you. As Shakespeare so aptly put, "It is much ado about nothing."

But for those of you who are on the path and who have opted for oneness, for allowing the knowing, intuitive nature within you to flow in balance and harmony with all life, the points made here and the means to access those points may provide some insight into the conscious awareness of our connected-ness, which is the Truth, even though we appear to be in separate forms. **Realizing the truth of one-ness or connected-ness represents a turning point in perception that will enable that part of humanity which craves home—a return to the greater Self in con-sciousness—to experience an abundance of miracles, magic, and**

adventure. Ironically, this turning of the tide of awareness is truly the only game in town, for, like the Hundredth Monkey Theory, which basically states that when enough energy changes direction, the rest will follow—we are embarking upon a new era of 1,000 years of peace, harmony, and abundant joy. Only those who are of a mind to receive this expanded vibration will be interested in this book.

In the case of my work, by signing up to be "me," I made a commitment to serve as a "safety net" for those who are consciously aware of their own contributions to the whole and who are dedicated to locating the avenue or awareness through which to express that dedication on planet Earth, as living examples. In signing up to be "me," I also agreed to be the space or awareness in which the change from *normal* (going along with unconscious habit energy dictated by outside influences) to *natural* (allowing the knowing intuitive nature within to flow fully) would occur. This change could also be described as moving from separation into one-ness, from darkness to light, and from bondage within the system to freedom of fully-supported Self-expression, which takes place individual by individual. It is in line with that commitment that this book has been written. We will all know when the tide has completely turned on planet Earth, for then both Acceptance and Gratitude will reign once again among all.

By the way, are we having any FUN yet?

Jeanie Lemaire
December, 1995

♡ ACKNOWLEDGMENTS ♡

As with all creative endeavors, no one person is endowed with all of the talents necessary to bring that creation to the public's eye. Therefore, I wish to take this opportunity to thank each and every one who took time away from their own interests in life to be available to me, to believe in me and my work, and to encourage me to share myself fully.

Initially, my thanks go to Richard Juarez. It was out of his love and support that I became aware of the need for such a book. I have been working with this information for so long that I had simply assumed it was in print somewhere. From his true inspiration and guiding spirit, I was able to manifest years of unfolding data in this book.

However, as many of my close friends know, I have a strong aversion to paperwork, and so I was encouraged to put a lot of the data on tape, which I did initially. At that point, I was blessed with the gift of Arlene Winters, who painstakingly listened over and over to those tapes to transcribe the data onto paper. I am still awe-inspired by such a commitment to my project.

Then the full title of the book was presented to me through the gift of a very special angelic Being named Melody Moore. From the beginning I was told, "The Body Talks . . . The Body Talks," and then one day, after her individual body session, she turned to me and said, "Why don't you call your book, "The Body Talks and I Can Hear It"?

Bingo!

After several more years of intense research through working with people across the nation, it was time to get down to work, so that I would have clear, concise material to give my friend and collaborator, Corinn Codye. A word is needed here to share about this Being. Corinn not only took on my project to edit, she also accepted it as her own, and made a commitment to see that the words used expressed my meanings fully and completely. Since I am truly "a fish in water" with this material, many times a fleeting word or phrase hinted at entire holograms of information that are so obvious to me in my world that I had taken for granted that all would understand. Corinn's gifted ability to sniff out the meanings, connections, and connotations *behind* my expressed thoughts, to ask me clarifying questions, to shape the creative presentation into a smooth flow and a consistent voice, and to weave through many of the additions that expressed themselves after the main body of the text was written, all helped to make the information much more complete, enjoyable, and accessible to the reader. Her wealth of knowledge and unending enthusiasm and encouragement, as well as her time and inspired contributions, were all given willingly and lovingly.

The next major character in this production is my good friend Richard Juarez again. I have been blessed by several Beings in my life who, for reasons I can't seem to understand, have a special affinity with that modern wonder, the computer. For this particular contribution, my thanks go to Rich. As I really got into the process of organizing my thoughts, he transformed the many handwritten pages into the printed word and saw that Corinn received the data on computer disk.

Then, I was hard-pressed to figure out exactly what I would want for a book cover about a topic of experience that's basically invisible. My thanks goes to Cate Cummings for unwittingly coming to my rescue. The cover for the second book, *BEING * Human & Divine Through Magical, Mystical Awareness *,* kept coming into view, and I almost settled for that image for this, the first book. But Cate suggested "overlays" of the Being's members (developed in the book) and out of that awareness came the actual artwork for the cover.

And so, a very special thanks also goes to my friend, artist Rachel Harwell, for the book's cover. To translate an invisible idea into form is a major miracle to me, and Rachel carried it off beautifully. Her work is gaining vast recognition for its most creative splendor, designed to engage the heart with our return to the light of pure consciousness.

I have one more acknowledgment to give, and that is to all of the incredible people with whom I have had the very real privilege of working. You may have noticed here on planet Earth that no matter what biological or legal ties we have to bind us, you can't make someone share their innermost thoughts and feelings with you. I, indeed, have been blessed many times over with the awe-inspiring one-ness of truly merging with another. To all of you, who have enriched my life beyond any material definition, I give my heart-felt thanks.

♡ EDITOR'S NOTE ♡

I wish to take this opportunity to thank Jeanie Lemaire for her life and her work, for her eternal presence as a friend, for her irrepressible humor, and for the privilege of helping to bring out the ideas contained herein. Jeanie plays her part in this life as the truest of human allies to all her clients—indeed, to all she meets—for she strives to live her message one hundred percent of the time, as a Living Example for people to "muster up to their Magnificence." She has, through her unique work, provided many with an experience they never had before: that of hearing, feeling, and completely experiencing, even for one moment, with heart, body, mind, and soul—the true, full backing that the Universe has for each of us—which is one hundred percent of love, support, and worth, one hundred percent of the time.

Jeanie once shared a story with me. She had asked a client to list all of the people who they felt were in support of them. However, she noticed wonderingly that her own name was not included in the client's list. Not being one to let a quandary go unattended, she inquired why. The person responded, with tears in their eyes, "Because you live with me, inside of me."

Speaking as a client as well as a friend of Jeanie's for many years, this book will undoubtedly prove a vast help to those with whom Jeanie has worked, for it will help them recall, process, and truly capture or internalize the "journeys" through which they have been led during their personal body therapy sessions. Because a few hours goes by so quickly and so much information is shared during a single session, the conscious mind rarely retains it all for handy review. Only through this book will many realize the actual extent of true help and the high dose of universal, practical truth that they have received, or appreciate the extent of real shifting of awareness that has taken place within them in a relatively short time.

For all other readers, this book provides both an inspiration and a map for meeting one's Self in a most delightful, heroic journey, with hilarious fun, gasps of Self-recognition, and wonderment at every step of the way.

Corinn Codye

The soul is not more than the body,
And the body is not more than the soul,
And there is no object so soft but it makes a hub
for the wheel'd universe.

—Walt Whitman, "Song of Myself"

If we are, we are wanted, and have the precise properties
that are required. That we are here, is proof that we ought to be here.

—Ralph Waldo Emerson

♡ INTRODUCTION ♡

No matter what your belief systems say, no matter what religious background you have, no matter what philosophical inclinations you follow, there isn't a human Being on the planet who doesn't see themselves as being located within a Physical body and, inside that Physical body, using thoughts and feelings to express that Self. Also, there isn't a one of us who hasn't been spoken to by our Physical form. In fact, you might say that our individual well-ness is in direct relationship to the least conversation from said body. So why is it that we have the cliché, "I am my own worst enemy"? Perhaps it is because we recognize that others may come and go in our lives, but we are always with ourselves. Therefore, we know what has physically occurred, we know how it looked to us, and we know how we felt about it. (Whether it was the truth or not is irrelevant to our perception of life.)

Now, regarding the Physical body, the medical profession has advanced great distances and uncovered cures and remedies to some pretty horrible ailments, for which we are all grateful. However, due in part to all the current wonders of modern medicine, many of us have lost track of what the Physical body is trying to tell us. In the course of my work, I have come to understand many of the messages that the Physical body tries to communicate to the rest of the members of the Being or Self.

For example, suppose you go out running for several miles, and when you come back, your left calf hurts.

Now at this point my comment to you would be, "Gee, that's too bad; how is your right calf?"

"It's just fine," you respond. "No problem. It's the *left* calf that hurts."

At this point, I really have to ask, "So, tell me, were you hopping on one foot or something? Because if it were just muscle strain, both calves would ache, wouldn't they?"

Then you respond, "Well, what else could it be but a pulled muscle?"

And my answer is, "Well, it is that, but by the way, are you by any chance concerned over some future emotional issue?"

You pause and say, "Hmmm. I don't know why you ask, but my divorce will be final in three weeks—and I didn't even want the divorce!"

I say, "Believe it or not, that emotional issue—the feelings about your divorce—is stored in your left calf area, and it has weakened your muscle strength. So when you went out to run, the left calf gave way to ache and pain."

And you whisper, "*Really?*"

In the above scenario, the Physical body was literally keeping the Being from freely moving ahead as long as its voice hadn't been acknowledged and "heard" by the *whole* Being. In other words, until the Physical, Mental, and Emotional body members are fully present and acknowledged as team players, our full "Self"-expression, connected-ness, and abundant flow in life will be impaired, and our ability to experience totality, unity, and freedom will be hindered.

The Physical body is our most solid, concrete means of expressing the Being who we are, in third-dimensional living—the next two closest expressions being the Mental and Emotional bodies. The Physical body just wants to be heard and is designed to give us our final warning before going into dis-ease. Prior to its announcement of our lack of attention on a particular matter, we have quite likely received Mental and Emotional opportunities to handle this lesson. So, by the time the item reaches our Physical form, it brings our awareness right before our very eyes, so it can let go of things that are no longer needed by us. Unlike the Mental and Emotional bodies, the Physical body passes no judgment and simply wants to realign the issue before it automatically shuts down to handle the situation itself, and it will *make* itself heard if we ignore it for long.

Many of us are familiar with the saying, "A cold will last either two weeks or fourteen days," meaning that no matter how much rest, fluids, and aspirin you take, the body will regroup on its own time—but have we ever stopped to consider what our Physical bodies are regrouping and recouping from? It is pretty much common knowledge that stress is the number one killer in life, affecting all of our body functions and resulting in many diseases, and we are all aware that potentially stressful situations exist all around us. What we have forgotten is that there are ways to alleviate this stress by allowing the Physical form to work with its partners, the Mental and Emotional bodies, to do what they do naturally—HEAL us.

Again, what we generally haven't realized is that, unlike our thoughts and feelings, the Physical body does not pass judgment or seek to rearrange any of the information it is receiving; rather, it is our storage area for all stages of our life lessons—the ones we have learned, the ones we are learning, and the ones we have yet to learn. And, rather than pass judgment or evaluate experiences, it simply and constantly rejuvenates, cleanses, and releases unwanted items, among other functions, to the best of its ability. It is my understanding that at the end of approximately seven years, the Physical body has fully replaced itself, down to the cellular level. Some areas, like the blood, are filtered constantly, while internal organs, cells, membranes, and other structures require more time to replace themselves. Plus, we have forgotten that we are not our Physical form *or* our thoughts *or* our feelings, but that rather we are the *Self* expressing through those avenues.

Unknowingly, a great many of us have lost the essential communication channel between our Self and the body we inhabit. That is, we have three dense bodies (Physical, Mental, and Emotional) through which we express the Self—or Being, or Essence, or Spirit, or whatever you call the spark that brings humans alive. And, until we re-connect our Self through all our bodies, we are truly operating at our own expense.

So what is this Essence or Self? We know that it cannot be what we eat, for in that case all those who ate the most would be the most energized. And if sleep were the Self, then those who slept the longest would be the most alert. Even our breath doesn't quite define it, as anyone who has learned controlled breathing can tell you. Much to our chagrin, we find that upset, depression, and lack of energy can still seep in at times.

So what exactly *do* we know about this Self or Essence, and how do we tap more of it for ourselves? Even though we are all born, live our lives, and die, we each have a slightly different approach to this thing called Life, to that which provides for individual perception and expression of the life-giving force. We do know that we, the Being, sense and view Life and our Self in Mental, Emotional, and Physical terms, and all three of these bodies are constantly informing and communicating with the Self, except when one or more of these channels is blocked. What I have come to recognize through my work is that people often have fewer than all three dense-body communication channels open and fully functioning at any given moment. If one or more of the members is impaired, shut down, or excluded completely from its access to the Self, eventually the excluded member *will be heard from*—in what may appear to be an extreme and painful manner (such as an ache and pain in the left calf!), in an attempt to restore the full flow of communication.

On the other hand, if one member, like the leg of a three-legged stool, is over-emphasized, by being more developed, it becomes larger than the other two, and again the ability of the person to be fully "gotten" is lost, for that member's voice overpowers the other two. In general this produces a frustration, as felt by us. For example, the child who is put ahead in school due to precocious intellectual development often finds themselves out of the first pick for team sports because their Physical form is less developed. Then, Emotionally, they may be teased by their peers because their actions are more "childish," and thus they decide to withdraw from social interactions. These Physically and Emotionally-experienced "slights" can result in low self-esteem or feelings of not belonging, and therefore a sense of alone-ness and lack of support.

But rather than just tell you about this, how about going on a little journey with me? This journey is into the inner realms of each of our Being-ness, into uncharted waters that will look different to each and every one of us. One common factor will prevail, however—that we are all connected and that each of us is whole and complete in our capabilities to enjoy a fulfilling life. In other words, all Life is merely vibrating, pulsating energy that simply vibrates at different rates, and incredible as it seems, the energy that we call our "Self" is a universe in itself. Each of us is in charge of our own universe, our perceptions, our beliefs, and how we hold the world, our "Self," and each other. Even more incredible, this universe we call our "Self" is synonymous with and in synchronicity with the universe in which we all live. Otherwise stated, not a one of us has to make anyone *do* anything. Rather, it is up to each of us to align our energies through our interests, natural talents, and sense of Self. Not a one of us views this life experience from exactly the same perspective, yet like spokes in a bicycle wheel, **we all come from the same core of full Acceptance and Gratitude**.

Because of this connected-ness, there truly is no new information available that on some level we don't already know. The trick, however, is in experiencing *conscious* access to that information and integrating our findings within the Self, so that we fully experience our Magnificence.

We each view the core or hub or wholeness from a uniquely personal perception of how to reach it. As we focus our attention on our individual lessons, we enrich others by being a Living Example to others of what is possible while being in human form. Our own expression of wholeness reaches others **through acceptance and gratitude** in discovering that there are as many ways to live a fulfilling life as there are humans to create it. You may have noticed that while some people have no difficulty at all with weight and can eat as they wish without gaining a pound, others have to battle the scales constantly, which reduces greatly the joy of eating and fills them up with guilt and shame. In the same manner, one person may keep on purchasing cars that continue to break down, while another has little or no trouble in the way of needing repairs. And how about the person who can't seem to stay with one job very long, while someone else celebrates thirty years or more with the same company? None of these scenarios are better or worse in themselves; it is how we hold them that has impact in our lives.

We are all here to learn lessons, which means there are unknowns to be explored, risks to be taken, adventures to be had—none of which can deter or change our individual Incredible, Magnificent, Priceless nature, which is so, simply by our being in form. All of the circumstances we experience are designed for our personal portion of the oneness or wholeness, in order that we might grasp specific lessons. So, it is not for us to say, "This here experience is *good*, but that experience over there is *bad!*—for if it weren't here to be experienced, it wouldn't be on the planet at all. At the very most we might say, about others, "Gee, I'm glad I don't have *that* particular lesson." But not a one of us, rich or poor, old or young, is without lessons to take back to the totality that we all are. So you see, we can ask advice and even hope for someone else to make our choices and decisions for us, but advice from someone else doesn't always help, because of our different lessons to learn and different natural talents for learning those lessons. So, if you ask me about something that isn't one of my lessons, I might easily sound flippant and say, "Just do this, that, and the other thing, and it will all be handled—what's the problem?" On the other hand, if the lesson happens also to be one of MY lessons, I am much more likely to have more compassion and empathy for your situation and feel more connected.

Also, the difficulty with giving advice, even though one speaks from experience, is that the person who is receiving the information has no "place" or fertile ground in which to put it, because they have no *experience* with which to connect it.

Regardless, ultimately it is up to us to "do" our own life, because I signed up to be me, and you signed up to be you, no one else. As they say, there is only one train leaving from the station, and you are either on it or not. You either participate or you don't; you either grow or die.

As hard as it is for any of us to fathom, no one is quite as interested in our own life drama as we are, no matter how exciting or traumatic the circumstances appear to us. Each of us directs our own play, while our own plays naturally cross paths with others' plays all the time, in perfect orchestration for the various lessons being lived and learned by the interwoven characters.

When it comes down to learning about our own Magnificence, the experience is like exercise. It's pretty much common knowledge that moving the Physical form helps to maintain wellness. However, *how* you move it is up to you—you can walk, swim, ski, exercise at home, go to a gym, jog, sky dive—do it all on one day, a little each day, or once in a while. After you have exercised and you feel better or stronger, you can use your understanding of the situation to see that you exercise again.

The same is true of valuing or fully backing your personal worth. You can read about it in books, go to seminars, and learn about it from a Mental standpoint, but until you start to put the principles into practice in daily life, all the information gathered is at a loss, for it has no experience to connect to, and this is why we can say that "words are cheap." Memorable quotes, such as those at the beginnings of chapters in books, fall into the same category, because in order to fully "get" their meanings, they need to have fertile ground to grow in, which soil is provided by the Emotional body, the part of us that actually "experiences" life.

The good news is, when you *do* have an experience that consciously connects you (the individual self) with You (the greater Self), any number of techniques can help to further your awareness, and that's where books, quotes, seminars, and so forth come in. As individual aspects of the whole, we reach that whole from many different directions, and this book is only one of those directions. Some reach it through many avenues, and others find just one that suits them. It all works.

So lean back, relax, and allow your own creative juices to flow, experience, and interpret the upcoming journey for you. For, as already noted, only you will live your whole life with you. Sorry, but all of the rest of us are destined to lesser roles in your production, your life experiences.

But cheer up, just remember that all of those people who thought they had a greater say in your life than you have, were merely embarked upon peripheral quests, and that in any given moment, full authority over the operational procedures of your life can be returned to you upon your request.

We will begin this journey by setting the stage for viewing it within the Self. As with all heroic adventures, this one is best received when it can be both experienced and observed, to provide an optimum integration of awareness. As such, we will travel together in this journey, in such a way that you, the reader, can both observe—by accompanying me into my reverie—and also participate—by dreaming, inquiring, allowing, and listening for the voices of your own Physical, Emotional, and Mental body representatives to make themselves known to you.

Indeed, I invite you to enjoy the play that is about to begin, and along the way have some FUN getting to know yourself, for we each have only our individual Selves to work with. A hundred stories about others can only hint at, without revealing directly, our own Magnificent uniqueness and inner Wisdom.

So, let the play begin. In any event, it's only conscious dreaming and not reality—or is it?

Every mind must know the whole lesson
for itself—must go over the whole ground.
What it does not see, what it does not live, it will not know...

—Ralph Waldo Emerson

♡ PROLOGUE ♡

IMAGINATION AND CREATIVITY

I'd like you to find a comfortable position, either lying down on a cushiony soft surface or seated in a comfortable chair, and let your Physical body melt into your niche. As you do, I'd like you to close your eyes and feel your muscles start to relax. Take a few deep breaths, letting them out with one or more great, long, audible sighs of relief, to release the breath and let it flow easily—as in "Aaaaaaaaaaaaahhhhhh . . . .," . . . "Uhhhhhhhhhh mmmmmmmmmmm . . . .," . . . and "Mmmmmmmmmmmmmmmmm mmmm . . . . !" . . . Yes, that's it, go ahead and vocalize if you can— it will help you to relax.

Now, if you would, I'd like you to envision a beautiful meadow. This is a very special meadow, for here the sun is shining brightly, but there are no harmful rays. You can also feel just the slightest breeze, allowing little, white, fluffy clouds to go by leisurely in the sky. And, as you look around, you can see that a carpet of wonderfully fresh, emerald-green grass is growing everywhere, covering the rolling hills. Be sure to take off your shoes and socks and feel the pure, virgin soil between your toes. As you look more closely, you can see and smell the sweet, delicious fragrance of the vibrant wildflowers, some of which have multicolored petals and are interspersed among the blades of grass. There are even some trees in this magical meadow, which cast inviting patches of shade, and some of the trees have crystal clear ponds next to them.

So, now, I'd like you to find a spot where there is quite a lot of the thick, beautiful, emerald-green grass growing, either in the sun or the shade, and lie down on your back, feeling the cushiony, soft support of this natural comforter of grass.

Now breathe in the brilliant, emerald-green color: breathe it in through your nose and mouth and all of your skin. Breathe deeply of this wonderful green, as if it were a liquid you could drink with every pore, every cell. Feel the soothing, healing fluid completely fill the Physical form—feel it spread as you draw it upward with your breath—up through the feet, calves, and thighs, to the buttocks, up through the hands and arms to the shoulders—and also up the torso from the tailbone to the neck, feeling the soothing, healing, green liquid flow in and around the internal organs, and finally bring the refreshing fluid all the way up to the top of your head.

Then swirl the soothing, green fluid around inside your Physical form, and slowly breathe out. As you exhale, let the swirling liquid absorb and carry away any thoughts you are having, any tensions that are just lying around loosely, and let the whole mixture flow back out through your hands and feet, right into Mother Earth, to be absorbed and recycled.

Then, with an even fuller breath, once again bring the healing, emerald-green fluid into your body, drawing it up through the legs, the arms, the torso, and as before all the way to the top of your head. Once again, swirl the liquid around and around, and just like in a test tube, as you go to breathe out, simply let your whole body drain right into the ground.

Now, please, simply unzip your skin and let your Essence out! By "Essence" I mean the awareness that you call "I" or "me," and that I would call "you." We could also call this awareness the Being or Vibrating

Energy or Soul or Aliveness—by any name, it is the conscious awareness of your own presence. For some, this Essence might be similar to the Physical form but more ghost-like or iridescent. To others, it might be a sense or a feeling rather than an exact picture. In any event, I want you to look back and see your Physical skin-suit lying on the grass—and be sure to check that your Mental thoughts and Emotional nature are left within that suit. This way, when you return to it to realign and reintegrate, all three of your dense systems will be available to you.

Now, to test your present state of awareness, I am going to ask you, the Being, to take what has only the barest hint of an arm and leisurely raise it up and easily touch the clouds. At the same time, take what only vaguely resembles a leg and in turn let this energy stretch way down, deep into the earth, past limestone, underground springs, and crystal formations. Now, as you bring both these hints of form back to your luminescent Self, I ask you to remain in this beautiful, peaceful meadow, where all things are possible, as I share my story with you.

The essence of Life is Self-organization.

—Fritjof Capra, *The Tao of Physics*

The moment is more accurate than anything we have been taught.

—from *The Right Use of Will*

♡ CHAPTER ONE ♡

IN THE ETERNAL MOMENT OF NOW

(From within a flowing void, as in a cosmic commotion or swirl of vibrating energy, having awareness of me and my "Self," yet without noticeable form or distinguishing marks, in this, the Eternal Moment of Now, from this space of totality and wholeness, I begin my story . . .)

The Being: *(formally, with a sense of full Self-proclamation)* To begin my story, I'd best introduce myself. Well, I am Me. . . . Oh—let's see, that doesn't tell you much, does it? Okay, how about this: I'm not from this planet.

(silence, deep as the sound of one hand clapping)

The Being: *(thrown off base, with a slight quaver in Its Self-confidence)* Oh dear, that won't work—that's like saying my astrological sign is LIBRA.

(after a pause) Now I've got it: I am not my body—but I have one to live in, and it's in decent shape, from all I can tell.

(curious silence, as energy begins to stir)

The Being: What kind of shape, you ask? You know, human—female, decent. *(pause)* Uh oh, I can see that's not enough information yet. Well, I do have an *elvian* nature—observant, playful. . . . I guess you might even say *mischievous*. Does that cover things for you?

(Sslence . . . somewhere short of fully grasping)

The Being: Well, don't get huffy.

(deep sigh)

The Being: *(starting to feel exasperation)* This sure is a pickle I'm in! You see, it seems so easy to me; but then, of course, I'm like a fish in water.

(agitated silence)

The Being: *(genuinely amazed)* You've not heard about the fish in water!? Where have you been all these years? I thought everyone knew that one!

Anyway, a fish in water is asked, "How's the water?"

The fish looks left, then right, then above and below itself, and replies, "What water?"

(continued puzzled silence)

The Being: *(just short of losing it)* You don't get it?—*(mumbling to Itself)* And I thought I was slow! *(aloud again)* Well, let me explain. To the fish, who is surrounded by water, the liquid is not separate. So, a fish-in-water statement is one that is obvious to you—a given, an "of course." In other words, it fits in with your belief system so well that you no longer think of it consciously. . . . *(trying to find a way to express the idea)* . . . Let me see . . . .

(the silence finally breaks, as sound penetrates the Being, and It hears a cough, as if a throat had been cleared—yet It had not even swallowed)

The Being: *(a bit unnerved, tentatively questioning)* Who's there?

(the sound becomes a Voice)

Voice: *(in full resonance)* Your Physical body representative.

The Being: *(with total disbelief)* My *who*?

Voice: *(fully confident)* Your Physical body representative. I've come to assist you in your dilemma.

The Being: *(still put out and with growing confusion)* But I can't see you!

Voice: *(a bit miffed)* That's not my fault. It's not like I haven't tried to get your attention before now.

The Being: *(attempting to recover Its composure)* So how did I activate you just now, so that I can hear you?

Voice: *(realizing there was no malice of intent)* Vague as you were, in your attempt to describe yourself, you came quite close to expressing your "Self," and "I" became more available to you than when you have tried to reach your "Self" through various other techniques.

The Being: *(feeling at last some common ground, and regaining Its pompous attitude)* Well, thanks a lot! Just because I can't sit still and focus my thoughts when I try to go within to find Self-guidance, that shouldn't keep you from me, should it?

Voice: *(with a chilly tone)* It's hard to say. I just store your life experiences. It's not my job to interpret them.

The Being: *(whining and whimpering)* I'm doing my best, you know. But it's not easy to fully "get" myself across to my Self!

Voice: *(reassuringly)* I can remedy that. But first I must say that you were rather vague in describing me just now. Perhaps I can help by describing to you the attributes that are under my jurisdiction. Then you can pick a vision representing all of these aspects to you—one that you can see and interact with.

The Being: *(intrigued and no longer feeling totally alone)* Okay . . . lead on.

Voice: *(shifting into full "teacher" mode)* You see, as your Physical body, I am a witness self. What I mean by that is, unlike the Emotional body and the Mental body, who are less dense than I am and therefore more aware of a need to protect their vantage points, I don't pass judgment. I simply observe, store, and retrieve when asked to, all of the experiences that you have.

The Being: *(with rising agitation)* Wait a minute! What is this about Mental and Emotional bodies? Just who are you, anyway?

Voice: *(with perfect and deliberate elocution)* As I said in your audio receptors, I am your Physical body representative, and I believe that I can assist you in describing yourself, if you would stop and listen for just a moment. The other two members whom I mentioned work very closely with me, and it is through us (your individual team) that others experience you, the Being, who lives inside of me. That's why you can't see the "me" who is talking.

You don't think I work alone, do you? In daily life, you are constantly interacting with all three of us. When we are in communication with each other, you have a great day. When we are at odds with each other, you, the Being, can't get through and Self-express. This produces anger, upset, and resentment, which builds up if it is not released, and you end up in dis-ease.

The Being: *(with renewed skepticism)* So why haven't I "heard" you before?

Voice: *(in a huff)* Well, it hasn't been because I didn't try to get through! Let's just say your listen-ability has been impaired, and leave it at that. I now ask that you take this eternal moment of now and hear me out. Then I will answer more questions, if you have them. Agreed?

The Being: Sounds good to me, "mon." *(chuckling at Its own joke)*

Voice: *(regaining a professorial tone)* As the Physical member of your foundation team, I am in charge of strength (both inner and outer), flexibility, and trust, both of yourself and others. Like the Emotional body, I live in the moment. For example, if you stub your toe, all of your attention immediately goes to your toe. You physically hit whatever the barrier is, then the impact of it reaches your awareness with feelings of pain, and next you ask, "What was that?" or you register in your mind, "I just hit a crack in the sidewalk."

All of these things appear to happen simultaneously, but actually, they occur a split second apart. So you see, I, as the densest system, have the final say in what you focus on. When you experience a pain in your back, that awareness infiltrates your daily activities—maybe even impairing you from some activity like a game of golf. At the very least, the pain will register on your face or show up in your voice as you go about your day.

I am designed to last for the duration of your life in full working order, which means, ideally, without announcing any mechanical breakdowns (limited motion, illness, or disease). Therefore, when I speak with an ache or pain, or send the Emotional body's signal of distress in the form of depression, sadness, or hopelessness—or am impaired by the Mental body's overzealous control of the situation with concerns of right, wrong, guilt, or judgment—then you might want to listen, because all of these responses indicate that you are out of balance—at-a-tilt—viewing life from a place of "separate and isolated" from your "Self" and the world around you. If I don't get a response to release this build-up, I will eventually become ill—sometimes ill enough to die to relieve the pressure.

The Being: *(wailing and sobbing)* Why would anyone want to do that to themselves?

Voice: *(matter-of-factly)* If you took a survey, I think you would find that no one *wants* to do that to themselves. It's just that when your team receives conflicting messages, we get at odds and are unable to carry out your desires. Conflicting messages occur when either one member overrides another or when one member is ignored or missing from the process entirely. I refer to these conflicting messages as habit energy, actions that are repeated without conscious thought. In the early years, in the alpha state, before puberty sets in, we as children live in the moment; we allow our emotional natures to flow and thereby release any pressure before it builds up. That's why a child can be told six times to clean up their room and hear it as if each time were the first. In this case, the parent or adult gets all flustered, and the child only knows it has done something wrong. By the teen years, when the child has switched to the beta state, this same behavior is done mostly to aggravate the adult, not because they didn't hear the first request. But I'm getting ahead of myself. I'd like to begin by painting a picture for you in your mind's eye about me and my attributes, so that you can create a visual image with which to interact with me.

But first, continuing with my attributes, in the area of strength, it is my job to see that your individual Physical parts get exercised, that sufficient nutrition reaches each individual cell, that periods of rest are included, and that all systems are up to speed. All of that produces a visual picture of Physical strength—that which others view when they interact with you.

On the inside, I am called upon to give you the stamina to continue in life. I can't give you the desire—that's in the Emotional body's area of expertise—but I can respond with inner strength once the desire ignites my pilot light. As you've probably noticed, daily activity is highly repetitious. If you are not happy with your work, your relationship with your Self or others, or with your circumstances in general, the *oomph!* it takes to get up each morning begins to wane. Again, the Emotional nature, who is the connector of all energy and vibration, works with me to provide this flow of energy.

In the area of flexibility, my jurisdiction covers everything from the ability to stretch the form to the strengthening of your ability to adapt to growth and change. Just like a camera lens, your Being can focus on one small point or expand to include a panoramic view. Most of us prefer space and the freedom to move about, over a small cell. So it is up to me to see that you have freedom of movement, not just Physically, but Emotionally and Mentally as well.

Trust is the most abstractual area that lies within my charge, and I must say it gives me the most difficulty to maintain. Like the mighty redwood tree, it takes a lot of moments to grow a person's trust until it is big and strong, yet in the blink of an eye, trust can be cut down, no matter how long it has been growing, or no matter how long you've been married, for example.

Again, it is a bit hard to see the separate duties of the Physical and the Emotional bodies, because they both operate in the moment. In this case, the trust that we experience physically by expressing through our Emotional nature—with a kind look, a soothing voice, and a loving touch—has a feeling of warmth that accompanies it. And, just like our need for many kindnesses, trust must be redefined at each and every moment. Unfortunately, this means that when a breakdown occurs, trust must be rebuilt from scratch.

If I may use my reference to children again—they live moment by moment and don't focus on past hurts or occurrences or plan for future maneuvers, as adults do. Therefore, an integration occurs: they cleanse their Being and Physical form by emoting until they are through, and they are then open and ready for the next life experience. So it is easier for them to set aside pain and to love again, even trust again, after being beaten or told that they were unworthy. As adults— thoroughly immersed in the trappings of the Mental nature, which is past/future oriented—we usually operate out of the belief that it takes language to communicate, whereas most children respond first to unspoken communication—touch or tone—from the moment they arrive in baby form, long before language is ever understood. Again, this difference between living moment by moment (the alpha state) and focusing on past and future (the beta state), is why parents can get very frustrated telling their child to clean their room for the tenth time, and it still isn't done. The child, living and trusting in the moment, with only partial memory activation, gets distracted and hears each request as though it were the first, whereas the parent, in the beta state and with full mental capacity to remember (and also living mostly in the Mental domains of past and future), can't understand why their child hasn't followed through. Besides, as adults, the parents store these occasions as memory, and they can eventually build a thought pattern that they cannot fully trust their child. Interestingly enough, these breaches in trust tend to be other-directed, without a thought on the part of the parent to check and see whether their own words or actions match each other! In any case, as children, we don't make the change from living in the moment to focusing on the past and future until about puberty.

The same seemingly unresolvable dichotomy that we witness in the above example of parents and children occurs inside each of us as our own Emotional and Mental natures strive to hold their own on behalf of the Being. Our Mental nature, holding the space of past/future so that we as Beings can live in the current moment, also stores up items and issues that can be used against our vulnerable, Emotional body. Thus it too loses respect or trust of the Emotional body's ability to do its job and begins to override said body with judgments, criticism, negativities, and limitations, resulting in internal conflicts—which is why, when I, the Physical body, tire of carrying their upsets, I become weakened and cannot maintain well-ness.

The Being: *(downright angry)* Now, wait just a dog-gone minute.

Voice: *(in a bland tone)* Are you interrupting again?

The Being: *(not really caring)* I'm sorry, but I just can't believe that because my thoughts and feelings are not aligned, I'm going to be in physical discomfort.

Voice: *(quite amused by Its Self)* Doesn't fit your belief system, huh? Well, if this helps, I'm like an internal closet—somewhat like the closets in your house. When they are full and start to overflow, you can't shut the door, because things are falling out. Plus, when the closets are full, it's hard to get to the items that have been pushed all the way to the back of the closet and buried under the more recent arrivals. I'm the same way, storing up all your Mental and Emotional upsets so they can be acknowledged, retrieved, and released when appropriate.

For example, if I asked you if you still owned every piece of clothing that you have ever worn from the time you were a toddler all the way through adulthood, you'd think I was crazy, wouldn't you? Yet many people keep every experience they've ever had, stored within their Physical body, instead of doing an occasional internal spring cleaning to make room for new growth and change. Ironically, many of us still operate from childhood hurts and fears that have been stored in our subconscious, covered over with sadness and anger, and further sealed over by the Mental body's rationale, which is designed to protect us when it feels like our survival is on the line. These stuffed-away items, whether we know they are within us or not, are the juices that fuel our actions. After all, what else do you keep with you always, besides your Physical form? Everything else comes and goes . . . people, places, items, you name it.

The Being: *(pausing to ponder this new revelation)* I've never looked at it that way before.

Voice: *(back to business)* So, to summarize my functions—as your Physical body representative, I am in charge of your inner and outer strength, plus the domains of flexibility and trust, plus the witness function of storing and retrieving all your life's experiences.

So now, perhaps you'd like the opportunity to allow a visual image of me, your Physical body representative, to surface. If you would, then I'd like you to close your eyes, take a deep breath or two, and relax—while I reiterate my attributes one more time. This time, as your inner Self hears them, please give yourself permission to create an image in your mind's eye that represents all of these features and functions to you. This image may look like something in nature, or perhaps an animal, or even an abstractual configuration, quite unlike anything we have on Earth. The point is, as I speak, to let your imagination go to work rather than try to figure out any particular image. As I say, just relax and let your mind's eye present you with some kind of an image. Here we go!

(reciting its attributes again briefly) I am your Physical body representative and a member of your personal team, which was designed for you to express through.

(pause)

I am also a witness, and as such I do not pass judgment on any of your experiences. I simply store these many moments throughout the Physical form until you ask me to retrieve or release them.

(pause)

I am in charge of three areas of your development—first, strength—both inner and outer; second, flexibility; and third, trust—both of yourself and others.

(pause)

And now, I ask you to share what image comes forward for you when you envision these attributes.

The Being: *(after a long pause)* Well, *(tentatively)* . . . at first I was a bit scared, because I didn't see anything. But then, as I repeated your statements in my mind, all of a sudden I saw this big cat—I believe it's the jaguar. I could feel its strength and agility—and, when I looked in its eyes, I felt I could count on it . . . trust it. Kind of crazy, huh?

Voice: *(appearing now before the Being as a Jaguar and purring softly)* Not at all. I am often envisioned as a member of the animal kingdom, but not always. So, please let yourself see me as speaking to you through this jaguar. I hope you can tell that I am friendly!

The Being: *(with a smile)* Oh, yeah. You just came over and laid at my feet, like a pet.

Jaguar: *(getting used to its form)* Very well. But we are not finished yet, for I am only one of your three foundational team representatives. So, who would you like to create next—the Emotional or the Mental member of your team?

The Being: *(without much thought)* My curiosity says let's hear about the Mental body.

Jaguar: *(responding enthusiastically)* Sounds good to me. First of all, understand that the Mental body member, unlike the Physical and Emotional, is *never* in the moment. I use that term— *never*—specifically here, because the Mental nature's gift is its ability to go *way* into the past and *way* into the far future— even the immediate past and the immediate future—but *never* into the momentary experience of *now*. In other words, as soon as I speak, the thought has already occurred. Going back to my example of stubbing your toe on a crack in the sidewalk, it appears as though the impact, feeling, and conscious aware- ness of what happened all takes place at once. But the times of having the thoughts and of actually voicing those thoughts differ. In the same way, when you talk *about* your feelings or your life, you cannot be presently "in the moment." So, one of the Mental body's most fascinating qualities is that it holds the space in which we are *aware* that we are "in the moment" of our lives.

Thus, the Mental member expresses as a connecting cord, providing our lives with a sense of continuity. Indeed, if we were momentary creatures only, then we wouldn't know where we are going, how we got to where we are, or who we love, where we live, what we drive, and so on. The Mental body remembers all the lessons we have learned, records the ones we are currently learning, and leaves open the possibility of lessons yet to be learned. And, since these lessons are in turn stored in the Physical form, you can begin to see how we three interrelate for your benefit.

Also, the Mental body representative carries the ability to gather in and store information and data. It can even analyze and figure out data, but it may surprise you to learn that the Mental member is not here to judge. Whenever it judges, limits, negates, or criticizes, it is doing the work of one of the other systems (most often that of the Emotional body). What the Mental member does excel at, however, is *creating thought*—taking unlimited vibration and energy, and gathering some of it together in a particular fashion, so as to appear to the Being, living in the Physical form, as an idea. So, besides its strength of holding fond memories, the Mental body representative also creates wonderful dreams and visions. Plus, it is up to the Mental body member to see that all thoughts and ideas reach the Being. After that, whether those thoughts and ideas are acted upon or not, is not the Mental's concern.

And, very important, along with all this, the Mental member happens to be the Being's number one cheerleader. It is designed to *back* the Being or Self, along with the other two members, one hundred percent, and I mean *one hundred percent*, of the time. Now, I really want you to hear me on this—it's not just a good idea.

Next, the Mental body also houses *knowledge,* everything that comes to us through learning and experience, and it houses one of the two healing factors given to each and every one of us to help lighten our load in life, and that is the gift of *forgiveness.*

When someone says, "I forgive you, but I can't forget what you've done," that statement is inaccurate, because once the Mind truly forgives, it actually deletes that item from its memory banks, just like editing an audio or video tape or film, and then the item is *gone*—it is no longer retrievable and no longer the basis for your actions. And, since all human beings mess up (and oh, yes, some do a better job of it than others), there isn't a one of us who hasn't had the need to be forgiven or to forgive another. Forgiveness is a gift with three faces: "I forgive the World, the World forgives Me, *and* I forgive Myself." This healing gift of forgiveness has tremendous inportance, because it enables us to keep what is of value and to let go of the rest, both for ourselves and for the others with whom we interact, which in turn allows more room for growth and constructive change and opens the door for Emotional compassion as well.

So, why not take this moment to see how you might picture the Mental member of your team as you let it appear to you on your internal screen. Again, let yourself play back the criteria. Release your notion of reality, and let the creative juices flow. . . .

(pause)

What do you see?

The Being: *(quite amazed)* I see a wizard! He's old, with a long white beard, and a wizard's hat and cape . . . though I must say, this creature seems a bit impatient, or agitated.

Jaguar: *(curious, but not surprised)* Perhaps you might ask it what's the matter.

The Being: *(tentatively, in a rather shaky voice)* Okay. Wizard, how are you?

Wizard: *(without the slightest hesitation)* I'm upset. This process, it's so slow. Can't we get on with things? After all, we already know this. Those Physical and Emotional chairpersons drive me crazy. They are always hanging out in the moment and not getting anything accomplished. I try to hurry them along, but they don't appreciate my efforts. It makes me so mad!

The Being: *(quick to respond)* Wait . . . . I thought you were not here to judge or criticize.

Wizard: *(quite bored)* That's just what the *Physical* member keeps saying. Who put that big cat in charge, anyway?

Jaguar: *(purring)* Time out! Can you, the Being, begin to see why you are having trouble describing your Self? Here's at least one of your members who is not in agreement with the rest of your team. And, as this member has just pointed out, each member is a chairperson in its own right, each with a totally different area of jurisdiction.

By the way, Being, do you feel unappreciated a lot?

The Being: *(suddenly feeling exposed)* Yes, how did you know?

Jaguar: *(matter of factly)* Because your Mental member is viewing *all* of life from that position, of being unappreciated. Therefore, everything that comes from your wizard friend is going to have a slant of unappreciation to it.

The Being: *(after pausing to put some of the pieces of this puzzle together)* I think I am beginning to understand, Jaguar, what you are showing me. But perhaps you could tell me about my third team player and chairperson through whom I express myself, so I can get the full picture.

Jaguar: *(responding eagerly to the show of interest)* Be happy to. Like me, the Emotional body representative is *always* in the moment. I hate to keep repeating myself, but I emphasize the term "always" for a reason. Indeed, we (the Physical and Emotional bodies) are both in the moment at all times. For example, Physically, when no body part is achy or in pain, we say we are in good health. The same is true for the Emotional body. When we emote, we cleanse the system, just like a rainfall does to the land, which leaves us ready to receive more input. Therefore, the Emotional chairperson houses all of the cleansers—anger, laughter, tears, joyful singing, and fear—which express out through the Physical form. (*Fear* acts as a cleanser in the sense that it is generated in the Mental body but has to be released through the Emotional body.)

However, the emoting or cleansing function is only one of the main distinctions between the Emotional and the Physical natures. The most noticeable difference is that the Emotional body is the holder of the space of wholeness *as universe*, or universal Self, while the Physical body holds individual experiences as a full universe within itself, within a space of *appearing* as a separate and isolated aspect of the universe.

The Being: *(confused and boggled)* But how can all this go on at once? It sounds so contradictory.

Jaguar: *(reassuringly)* Not at all. As mentioned earlier, each person is whole and complete, with all of the means of experiencing a fulfilling life, and is solely in charge of that life. That wholeness or universal wonder, or life, is perfectly orchestrated to align with the entire universe in which we all live. So even as the Physical body is our densest system, it is also a complete universe in itself, capable of taking us wherever we (inside said body) wish to go. At the same time, for experiential purposes, our individual physicalities allow for many perceptional experiences, like the spokes on a bicycle wheel, and thus the *appearance* of separation within our universe.

(pausing briefly to confirm that this point has registered with the Being, who indicates understanding with a thoughtful nod)

Jaguar: *(forging ahead)* As the densest form, the Physical expresses or produces the Emotional body's thrust. At the same time, if you, the Being, don't feel safe enough to emote, that same Physical form will stuff away those feelings. Things eventually begin to get crowded inside the Physical form, as the emotions fester there.

(pausing again to watch the Being absorb this information)

The Emotional chairperson is also in charge of seeing that "created" thought—from the Mental body's jurisdiction—gets connected to physical manifestation—in the Physical body's domain. It provides the *oomph!* to get us where we want to go. It also provides the "knowing-ness" or the *value of connected-ness* to the greater Self or universe.

The Being: *(slightly confused by the unfamiliar expression)* Wait a minute—just what do you mean, "value of connected-ness?"

Jaguar: *(appreciating the Being's quandary)* I'm speaking of the degree to which any idea supports or connects to the greater wholeness. For example, when a person or company goes right from the drawing board—or thought, so to speak—to a physical product or service costing X amount, while by-passing the working conditions and lives of the people who actually create the product or who monitor the assembly line to see that the original instructions are followed, that person or company's efforts will always be to some degree separate from humanity.

On the other hand, any created idea that flows or is routed through the Emotional member will always serve humanity in physical form, because the knowable connection to "whole" reaches everyone on a deeply subconscious level. The reason is that love energy lives in the Emotional body, and love energy, situated in the physical part of our form called the Heart, is the connection of our individual knowing-ness to the oneness that we all are. In other words, when the Emotional body—being on-line with one-ness—backs an idea, the idea serves all of humanity and the world we live in. However, when that energy is at-a-tilt and focused solely on one individual's blurred vision or reality, disaster—i.e., violence and pain—can occur.

The Being: *(alarmed, looking confused and distressed)* But how can I recognize the difference?

Jaguar: *(in a confident, soothing purr)* For example, in an idea for a product—profit quotas, desired sales results, and innumerable graphs and charts, in and of themselves mean nothing! It's only when they get hooked up to actual production and delivery and consumption of any given item that they gain any significance. However, no amount of graphs, charts, good ideas, or desired results—even when hooked up with a finished product—means *anything at all* in the universal picture if it does not in some way enhance the quality of life for all on the planet. We as human Beings don't get up in the mornings, bother to make our beds, do the dishes, or go to work for no reason. We do so to experience living, not just surviving or repeating known tasks. Every moment of every day holds the *possibility* of being miraculous—of expanding our sense of "Self" and the world around us.

Since we spend a great deal of time "on the job," if, while there, we find no visible concern for our welfare, our contribution, or our enthusiasm, we are likely to become upset or withdrawn and very aware of our "separate" status, and then we will go to great lengths to protect our Self and our position that the job in question is not worthy of our full participation: we begin to come in late to work, just do a so-so job, take long lunches, or many times bad-mouth our bosses or company to others, and with this stance, all possibility of connected-ness and further Self-awareness goes right out the window. We stop growing and start dying.

To approach this idea of being connected versus disconnected, from another tack, say you were thinking about a trip to India, and you had figured out that you had X amount of time available and X amount of money to spend plus a list of specific items you wanted to see, exactly the perfect trip for you. Into that "created" thought, you also put what to take, when to get your ticket to have the best air fare, and what would need to be handled at home in your absence (i.e., bills to pay, plants to water, dogs to walk, and so on). You also noted what items you would need to purchase—clothes, toiletries, traveler's checks, suntan lotion, and so forth—and what shots to get, as well as to make sure your passport and visas were in order.

Now, whether this process took a day, a week, a month, or forever, no matter how detailed you got, would you find yourself in India at its conclusion? As you probably have noticed, not a one of these items actually happened. They are merely well-planned. So, hard as it is for the Mental body to "get" this fact, it is incapable of doing the job of its two counterparts, the ones who actually deliver you to your destination or produce the planned result. At the same time, just hopping on a plane headed to India without thinking the venture through could result in being sent home without a passport, getting ill from not being inoculated properly, not seeing everything that you would have liked, and perhaps not even discovering what was there to be seen. In any event, without the *connection* factor between the Mental body representative and the Emotional body member, which provides the energy to see that created thoughts, when desired, do get manifested physically—we are left without our most powerful expression of Self, which is having thoughts, words, and actions match, or, stating our Truth and following through on it. In other words, once awareness opens up or "hits" us, it must be connected with the momentary systems (the Emotional and Physical), to *solidify* the *validity* that we all are.

(Jaguar pauses to allow the information to register)

Does that help you understand the "value of connected-ness" that the Emotional member provides?

The Being: *(nodding appreciatively)* Yes, it's much clearer, thank you.

Jaguar: *(picking up where it left off)* The Emotional body also houses Wisdom, for Wisdom comes from "what we know that we know," not from what we have gathered in. For example, we all know when someone has put a loving hand on our shoulder as opposed to when it is one of anger pressing in. The same is true for tone of voice. A child, unable to talk, gets the gist of the conversation by listening to its tone, just like animals do. These things are knowable, part of our natural sensitivity and expression, and not something we've learned in school or life. If someone screams, "I love you!," you receive a mixed message. The words express an endearment while the tone proclaims, "You worthless piece of filth!" Your Emotional body reads the tone and receives the emotional expression that gives the force to the tone it perceived.

Like the Mental member, with its healer of Forgiveness, this body also houses a universal healer, and that is the gift of Laughter. Laughter is not only one of our cleansers, designed to remove bitterness and resentments, but it also alleviates Physical discomfort as well.

So, in your internal vision, how do you see this body member represented in form?

The Being: *(after a pause . . . full of awe and wonderment)* Oh, it's so beautiful—it's a baby deer. It's so precious and a bit shy. . . . I hope I don't scare it.

Jaguar: *(helpfully)* Well, why don't you ask it a question—so it can see you won't harm it.

The Being: Okay. *(with growing tenderness)* Deer, I am a Being who gets to communicate through you. How are you?

Deer: *(quite tentatively and more than a little scared)* Is it safe to come out? I get so fearful. I know I don't do things so well. I try real hard, but I am so sensitive to harshness and criticism. I know I should be stronger, but I can't help myself.

Jaguar: *(mildly moved)* Now this is interesting, isn't it. Here's your Emotional chairperson, appearing almost crippled. Do you, as a Being, sometimes feel inadequate?

The Being: *(startled, becoming slightly flustered)* Of course, doesn't everyone? I mean, I mess up, just like the next person.

Jaguar: *(pondering the scope of the statement)* Yes, well, doesn't everyone—it's often so. Only you must realize that you, the Being, are not balanced inside yourself if we three members are not fully operative and respectful of each other. Do you run away from situations that are uncomfortable?

The Being: *(exceedingly vulnerable)* Yes, but I can't help it. They scare me.

Jaguar: *(observing frankly)* And now your Emotional representative views everything through a basis of not backing its knowing-ness, which is compounded by the Mental body's desire to control you because it thinks you can't do your job! Makes it kind of hard to take risks in life, don't you imagine?

The Being: *(struggling between conflicting feelings of frustration and gratitude)* Yeah—so what do we do now? I can see by these images that how I interact with others is caught inside of me, and also that my team isn't supporting me. What can I do to change that? You've been most helpful for me to see the cross-purposes going on within me. I'm amazed at how you don't seem to be very affected by these cross-pulls.

But, now that I think of it, I'll bet that every time I have been under the weather (either sick or depressed), it was you, trying to get my attention. Am I right about that?

Jaguar: *(quite impressed)* You are a quick study. As the Physical body representative, all I can do is bring things to your awareness level. I can't work alone, and neither can the other members. As a team, we create wellness. When we attempt to work as independent agents, we create stress within you as well as without.

The Being: *(on the verge of being overwhelmed by the sudden impact of this awareness)* But how did I get to this point? I don't remember getting off track.

Jaguar: *(heading off into one of its favorite topics—human development)* That's because the track itself has been off-center for thousands of years. Just look to history and the many times when whole groups of people have been persecuted . . . or look at the physical upheavals of famines and plagues . . . or look at the amount of abuse and denial in various forms and how widely these have persevered throughout humanity. For example, look to the many ways we as a culture instill Physical, Mental, and Emotional limits to men and women, by reinforcing the belief that we are very different. In the female case, she's not accepted as physically able to be equal to man. What a misnomer. Remember the first Iron Man competition in Hawaii? There were fourteen participants, only one of whom was female. Then, after swimming several miles in the ocean, bicycling, and running a full marathon, the female came in fifth. That means only four males beat her times. Or how about women and intellect. Right now in our own U.S. House of Representatives and Senate, women are equal participants. So, females aren't just nurturers designed to raise children. And how about males: males who stay home to take care of family and home are popularly considered less worthy than a business man.

All of these aspects of off-centeredness over the years have produced fear and anger in humans, and in that state we separated from the whole of our Being-ness just trying to survive under terrible conditions. Well, over time, this built into unconscious habit energy for humanity as a whole, and we set up our social interactions to match the fear and anger that was building inside. Eventually, the accepted norm was to practically dictate how young boys and girls—and grown men and women—were "supposed" to be and act and live out their lives—heavily laden with guilt, shame, and blame. The final result of all this history was that no one grew up being allowed to naturally and fully Self-express.

It wasn't until the atom bomb was dropped and thousands of people were walked into gas chambers that all of what had been building throughout all this human history became critically altered. In fact, the masses of folks born right after World War II are commonly called the baby "boom"—an appropriate name, I think, since these Beings were not willing just to keep going along as usual. Plus, with technology advancing by leaps and bounds, change was definitely under-way—so much so that by today, issues and concerns which were once considered as incorrect to discuss in public or to handle openly are now common conversation and in general knowledge.

And yet, do you notice that where people come from is slow to shift? We are all so ingrained in the habit of putting up with things and with the idea that life will never change, that we sometimes quit trying, thereby proving ourselves right, and solidifying even further these limiting habit energies or un-conscious repetitive actions. For example, by focusing on the Physical forms and saying that men and women are more different than just their "plumbing" parts (i.e., elimination and reproductive organs), we have lost track of the fact that we are all human Beings—each and every one of us capable of achieving any goal, living any way, and working at whatever we choose—being assertive and nurturing, intelligent, and loving. Do notice I said human "Beings," not human "doings." Therefore we do not have to DO anything to prove our worth. Rather, it is up to each of us to "Be" our "Self"— expressing fully and clearly through these three bodies. When we are experiencing our Selves as human Beings, abuse will not be tolerated by anyone—children, women, minorities, or members of socio-economic strata.

Actually, we (humanity) now at least are gaining the awareness of what has happened in the past in terms of Mental understanding, but we haven't yet fully grasped the tools or experience to see that said new aware-nesses become actuality, which ability is within the jurisdiction of the Emotional and Physical bodies, and further, to see that these aware-nesses and experiences get backed *one hundred percent* by the Mental body.

The Being: *(devastated and slightly breathless)* I can see what you mean, Jaguar, for in my world I am the center and the driving force, and I've just seen how my own members are not working together. How can I ever hope the world will work, when I (and probably others) are out of kilter? It's a nice idea, all of this change—but no go.

        (the Being's hint of a form slumps dejectedly)

Jaguar: *(cheerily)* Well, the good news is that each of you, as Beings, can clear your internal systems and realign your members, but it will take a bit of work. *(pause)* Are you willing?

The Being: *(with a spark of renewed hope)* Oh yes, just lead me—er, us— in the right direction. I now know that you, as my Physical representative, cannot do it alone. I realize that I must clear and develop all three of you if I hope to balance my internal world. So, where do we go first?

Jaguar: *(glad for the opportunity to be of service)* Well, may I suggest that we all go together to attend a certain meeting that's just about to get under way nearby—the Human Body Parts Symposium. In fact, I was just on my way there, and I don't believe you'll find a better starting point than this particular convention.

If you'll all accompany me, I believe that, once there, we will be able to get a very clear idea of what kinds of information and life experiences are stored in me, the Physical form. At the very least, it will be a start in terms of awareness.

(compassionately) And I know that this news has been un-nerving, but take heart, because awareness after experiencing discomfort is the first step toward moving you and us out of any debilitating habit energy, or any negative, unconscious, repeated behavior that is not supportive of the Incredible, Magnificent, Priceless Gift that all of life is.

You know, I have always thought there should be a banner waiting for every baby coming out of the tube, saying, "Welcome, you Incredible, Magnificent, Priceless Gift! We are so glad you are here!"

(with a sly wink) Then again, most babies can't read—but the idea's great, don't you think? Just think of all the hassles you could have avoided if you had remembered from the outset that your personal worth is a *given*, that it cannot be lessened

in any way, and that you don't ever have to prove your value or match someone else's idea of what your worth is!

The Being: *(now fully caught up with enthusiasm)* Yes, Jaguar, the idea's terrific—and just maybe, if we human Beings can just get our members to develop and align, we might experience such a wonder!

Wizard: *(aside, muttering its suspicions to itself)* Hey, I haven't worked long hours all of these years to build sufficient protection around this Being for nothing! And look what kind of thanks I get! Just let them (my fellow comrades) *try* to loosen my hold, and then we'll just see what happens. After all, I have to protect my *right* to overshadow the other members, and even the Being itself, when necessary. The Being didn't put me in charge for nothing—and besides, I *like* running the show. Whether or not it has worked for the rest of them, I have always tried my best to protect the Being!

(aloud now, in a dazzling, calculated-to-impress display of its capabilities) As *I'm* the one who focuses on manifesting, I suggest we rally our energies together and really *intend* to get *all* our questions answered while we're at this Body Parts symposium.

(Jaguar, the Being, and Deer all cheer their hearty agreement, and then the company departs together quickly for the annual meeting of the Human Body Parts Symposium, which is just about to begin.)

Nothing alive can go unattended.

—Nora Roberts, romance novelist

♡ CHAPTER TWO ♡

THE ANNUAL SYMPOSIUM OF HUMAN BODY PARTS

(Jaguar, the Being, Deer, and Wizard have arrived at the Annual Symposium of Body Parts. They enter and begin to locate seats in a large auditorium that is filled to capacity with a boisterous crowd of symposium enthusiasts.)

Jaguar: *(with authority)* Okay, everyone. Let's all stick together, as there are many participants here today.

Deer: *(feeling trepidation)* Please don't lose me. I'm afraid of large groups of energy.

Wizard: *(testily, with barely subdued anger)* Not to worry. I can locate you easily, as you are the only timid Deer energy present.

Jaguar: *(attempting to soothe the growing tension between Deer and Wizard)* In any event, we'll make it easier on our Being if we can locate four seats together and do it quickly. The conference is about to begin.

(a Foot moves toward the podium)

41

Foot: (*surefootedly*) Quiet, please! . . . . Please, if you would, quiet down! . . . Thank you. As president of this year's Body Parts Symposium—and a foot to boot . . .

(*polite laughter among the assembled participants*)

. . . I'd like to welcome all of you various and similar body parts to our annual meeting. What a crowd we have this year! It looks as if almost all segments of the body are represented here today—and many by several examples. We are so thrilled to be holding this most prestigious event in . . . .

Head: (*screaming*) I can't take it any more—I just can't take it!

Foot: (*attempting to maintain order*) Excuse me, order please. If you would please take your seat . . .

Head: (*disregarding any reasonable input*) I can't! I hurt all of the time—I need help!

Foot: (*growing increasingly concerned that all of its efforts to orchestrate the symposium are approaching rapid disintegration*) Please, if you would just hold off commenting right now, we will get to complaints and possible cures in the afternoon session. By the way, who's talking?

Head: (*desperately*) I'm a Head, and I am pounding so hard, and the pressure inside . . . .

Foot: (*firmly*) Look, Head, we're all very sorry, but we've just opened the symposium and we have a whole calendar of events lined up . . .

Left Thigh: (*chiming in*) Hey, I hurt too. The bones in my thigh (get it right in print please, the *Left* Thigh) are ready to go on strike.

Right Thigh: *(highly irritated and not wishing to be outdone)* Well, what about me? . . . I, as the *Right* Thigh, have to carry your weight as well as my own when you don't feel up to it.

Left Thigh: No you don't.

Right Thigh: Yes I do.

Left Thigh: No you don't.

Right Thigh: I do, too!

Foot: *(shouting frantically)* Please, please, come to order! This will never do.

The Being: *(standing up on the impulse of a sudden inspiration and approaching the podium while addressing Foot)* Can I help?

Foot: *(in dazed disbelief of the situation)* And *who* are *you*?

The Being: *(inspired and enthusiastically sincere, even while marveling at Its own boldness)* I am Me, "a Being." I live inside of one of these complete bodies. Although you can see only a hint of me, I am very real and completely familiar with their di-lemma. You truly cannot quiet or ignore these parts for long. They do have the final say to my "Being" here, and that's true for all humans. I think I can help out, though, if you would allow me a few moments to address the assembly.

Foot: *(in a disgusted tone)* Okay, but hurry up. We have a full agenda of wonderful guest speakers.

(focusing again on those present in the auditorium) Order, order please! . . . *(the crowd begins to come to order)* We are going to change today's events and begin with an open forum—only don't all speak at once. I'm going to turn over

the podium temporarily to the charge of this Being, whom we can all hear and faintly see, so please be cooperative.

The Being: *(hesitantly at first, but with increasing conviction)* I had no idea that I'd be speaking here today, but I can say that I came to this symposium to help my team members, who seem to store upsets and unfinished business inside my Physical parts like all of you.

So, I would like to invite you to participate in a particular process that I am familiar with—and all of you Body Parts can join in—for I suspect we all will find that this will assist us in freeing up and releasing the stored issues that are blocking our duties and our ability to listen here today. I certainly hope to free up my own members to work together on my behalf! Fair enough?

(murmurs of assent from the audience)

Being: *(with buoyed assurance)* Great. So, I'd like you all to get comfortable in your seats—legs uncrossed, arms resting, eyes closed (if you have eyes)—and listen to my voice as I describe a scene. I want to remind you ahead of time that there are no right or wrong responses, and we are not here to harm anyone or any part of the body.

(the Being briefly pauses to allow the audience to comply)

♡ The Outdoor Amphitheater ♡

The Being: *(continuing vigorously)* I'd like you to see your Self—the inner awareness that each of you are—as if you were in the audience of an outdoor amphitheater. On the stage of this outdoor amphitheater, I'd like you to imagine two huge, twenty-five-foot-tall speakers that face in towards the stage—not away from it. The microphone to those speakers is set up in the audience, where you have easy access to it, about one-half of the way back from the stage.

Now, please allow your Self, whatever Body Part you are, to place down there on that stage *any person, any situation, and any item* that has not ever or does not currently support the particular Body Part that you are!

(pause)

In other words, just send up onto the stage whatever or whoever comes to mind from whom you recognize that you have not received *complete support and respect*—on the level at which you as a Being wish to be grasped—and I will do the same.

For those of you holding issues that need Emotional release—such as anger, fear, resentment, depression, and so on—place those emotions up on stage as well.

For those of you carrying Mental judgments, criticisms, or other concerns, be sure to put them on the stage too. I don't wish to hurry you, so please take your time and put up there on stage any items, any situations, any people, feelings or thoughts that have not or do not support the individual Human Body Part that you are. . . (and the Being that I am). . . .

(ten minutes pass with complete silence in the auditorium . . .)

How is it going? Do you all have every item, thought, feeling, situation, or being on the stage?

(a nod of Body Parts confirms that this is done, while the Being confirms that this is so within Itself)

Good. Now, I want to ask each of you to take this opportunity to talk *directly* to each energy that you have put up on your stage, and tell it *exactly* what's been *true* for you in reference to that energy. Please be sure to talk to each item, thought, and so on, directly—and do not worry about being kind. This exercise is designed for you to fully Self-express. So, if need be, moan, groan, holler, scream, yell, use nasty words, talk in tongues, or whatever helps you to release any and all built-up resentments and hurts. Please feel free to vocalize, as I am quite sure that this vibration helps cleanse the Emotional system. Otherwise, use your internal viewing screen to talk to each energy you have identified. You have ten minutes, starting now, to let it all hang out!

(mass bedlam unfolds as the Being also takes the opportunity to address Wizard, Deer, and Jaguar inside Itself, and all of the people, situations, and items held within these members' jurisdictions)

(meanwhile, in the auditorium . . .)

Jaguar: *(groaning)* Oh, my ears . . .!

Deer: *(shouting over the din)* I guess these Body Parts feel safe enough, because they all seem to be vocalizing.

Wizard: *(barking with annoyance)* I wish they'd just get on with it! I came here to get the information on individual Body Parts and what they store. We won't get anywhere without that information.

Jaguar: *(attempting to remain calm)* Hold on to your hat, Wizard. I'm sure we will all be able to receive more data once these delegates clear out some of what they've been holding on to.

If I'm correct in what I suspect, then at least they'll be able to listen, instead of just demanding to be heard.

Wizard: *(grudgingly)* Okay, okay. So patience isn't my long suit.

(nearing the ten-minute point . . .)

The Being: Please finish up. You have thirty seconds. . . .

(and, inside Itself, demanding in no uncertain terms that Its three members let go of old grudges and be open to growth as well as releasing old hurts and resentments from past experiences . . .)

(continuing once the noise level drops) . . . Okay, so who would like to share first?

(loud mass commotion . . .)

The Being: *(efficiently moving the process along)* Order, please. . . . Quiet! It seems you all have a lot to share, so let's ask just a few of you to share out loud, and then we can pair off and all share together. Okay, Left Arm—what do you want to tell us?

Left Arm: *(in incredulous enthusiasm)* I was so amazed! I didn't think anything would show up—but then, as you kept repeating what we were to look for, I began to feel so much anger and frustration built up inside me—it was a feeling as though I had simply been dismissed, as if my sharing to the rest of the body that I'm attached to wasn't important enough to be heard! And yet, all this time, as the Being in the body I'm a part of has gotten more and more stressed, I have reached a point where I just feel so heavy and tight that at night, when I usually rejuvenate, I can't sleep, and I spasm a lot. So, I put the Being on the stage, and then I put the built-up anger and minor frustrations up there too. Then I proceeded to tell all of them how unappreciated I felt and . . . and that I was pushed over my limit! I told them specifically where I felt they had dropped the ball in terms of supporting and including me.

When I finished, I felt so much lighter—and ready to work with my Being again! I'm so grateful to have had somewhere, some way, to off-load all that weight.

The Being: Thank you, Left Arm. So, now, how about you, Head? You've already told us of your physical pain.

Head: *(with tremendous relief)* It's a miracle! I can't believe it! As soon as you started talking, I began to empty out all the thoughts I've been keeping around just in case of rape or robbery or crime, and I sent them up onto the stage. I didn't realize how much of my energy was being used to ward off unknown fears. I ended up putting the Being who lives inside of me up there as well. He (my Being is a man) watches the news at least three times a day. He even goes to bed right after the news, with all of it fresh inside of me. No wonder I don't sleep. I'm always sure something's going to get me during the night, and that in the morning I won't exist.

I found these fears lurking around in my frontal lobe, in the base of my skull, and even in my memory banks. No wonder I was at my wits' end! The amassed fear was so great that I actually thought I was being eaten alive. So I told him *directly* that I would not put up with these unknown fears as my only thoughts for the day! And, lo and behold, he seemed to hear me, which has not been the case for a very long time. So, now I feel freed up. Thank you so very much, for now I feel free enough to be able to listen to what's going on here.

The Being: *(in full acknowledgment)* We are all pleased for you, Head. Congratulations are definitely in order. So, now let's hear from that Right Thigh who spoke earlier.

Right Thigh: *(appreciative at being remembered)* Thank you, Being. I didn't realize how much resentment I had built-up over the Left Thigh! It seemed to me that *it* was always under the weather, and therefore *I* was having to compensate a lot—until somewhere along the line I dropped my faith in *its* ability to do its job. Now I see that I haven't listened to any other input from it since I made that decision. I just decided that I had to go it alone for my Being, and it's left me bitter and unresponsive. Several times my Being has set out jogging and in no time at all I've let it be known that I wasn't interested in participating. I've felt so alone and unappreciated! So I told the Left Thigh, after I put it on the stage, that I didn't trust it any longer to do its job, that I was full of hurt and bitterness, and that I don't want to live that way anymore! I not only put the Left Thigh up there, but I put the Spine on stage, too—for not recognizing a block in the body's communication system! And then I put the Head up there as well, for not trying to set me straight. I even put myself up there for getting so far out of whack—I was so removed from what was important to me, which is just what my Being—she's a female—does a lot of the time. She's so hooked into being a "mom" and a "wife" and an "administrative assistant" that there's little time for her Self. So, I get full of these other people's experiences and I think, what about me and my Being—what about our personal growth and interests? We love doing for others—yet not to the point of loss of Self!

So, I saw this image of myself being high up in a tree and walking to the end of a branch and then starting to saw it off—in trying to be absolutely right as to how I "saw" things, . .

(a few whoops amid chuckles in the crowd)

. . . so that I lost track of other possibilities, lost compassion for the Left Thigh's dilemma, and made it my enemy—while forgetting that we were designed to work together to keep our Being mobile, and that it is so important that we support each other.

I even asked my Being for forgiveness for attempting to operate in such separation from the group. So, thanks to you, I let it all hang out and saw clearly, for the first time in a long while, my own part in my own upset!

The Being: *(amazed and intrigued)* That's quite a revelation, Right Thigh. So now, to get another point of view, let's have your Left Thigh respond.

Left Thigh: *(sharing excitedly)* Wow, am I impressed! You don't know how long I've been trying to get through to my right counterpart. In fact, I had no idea why the Right Thigh hated me so much—but I could feel it. I've always tried so hard to do well, but it has felt like an uphill climb. Our Being had a very difficult and abusive childhood, and I seem to be the spot where she carries a lot of those old wounds. But, like a closet, I too can get full and not be able to take in any more. As a result, whenever that happened, there would go all of my strength towards survival. I tried several times to let both the Being and the Right Thigh know what was happening, but it seemed to me they were both in denial, saying, "Just do your job and shut up!"

Well, eventually I just got exhausted and gave up. That's what I put up on the stage—pure exhaustion. I'm so tired, I could sleep for a week. I also put what I called *a lack of compassion and an unawareness to my needs* on stage—and I told them I'm tired of always being told what to do and not being included in the decision-making process or supported in my own arena. Even *one* thank you from the Being would have helped! I could see the Being's dilemma and felt sympathy for her. But I didn't feel like *I* should be the one who has to receive and store the bulk of her upset. Even I lose trust in the moment, if too many times the rug has been pulled out from under me.

The Being: *(fully acknowledging the Left Thigh's and all the other shared realizations)* Thank you, Left Thigh. It is amazing just how much each of you individual Body Parts have experienced. I'm sure we could hear from everyone, but Foot has asked me to complete this process so we might move on to today's agenda. I encourage each of you now to find a partner and take two minutes each to share your experience . . . starting now!

(four and one-half minutes later, as the buzzing begins to die down . . .)

The Being: *(bringing the process to completion)* Okay, please thank each other, and I ask you again to relax and focus as we finish up with this exercise, for it is not enough to clear out these misnomers, leaving an empty space; rather, it is most important to fill that space with items that nurture and work for you. So, I want you now to use your imagination to create whatever form works for you to dissolve the stage that you have just been using, along with everything on it, plus the audience area, and be left with nothing but pure, virgin earth. For example, you could use fairy dust or a magic wand to dissolve the images. Or, you could create a huge ball of white light and have the scene all merge with the light. Or, you could slice and dice and bury it all deep within the earth to absorb and recycle. These are just a few ideas you can use—or you can be wild and create your own. I want to see an indication, by any slight movement in your chair, of when you are done and ready to move on. Each of you has about five minutes to completely demolish your inner auditorium, down to the point of virgin, uncultivated soil . . .

(a short while later . . .)

The Being: *(feeling quite satisfied with Its new inner landscape and moving ahead to the final step in the process)* Okay, now I want you again to get those creative juices flowing and plant, in your newly-prepared, virgin soil, everything that nurtures you. You are welcome to plant waterfalls and mountains, flowers and vegetables, peace-joy-and-love, or whatever supports you absolutely, making sure you see a form for each item that is firmly planted in the soil. No one else may venture here without your express invitation, and even then, you can wish them away if they don't behave themselves. And, any time you feel isolated or separate, you can come to this beautiful spot and be replenished.

(complete, absorbed silence)

Know that you can revisit and add to your image of this spot or change it whenever it suits you to do so. I'll give you a few more minutes to visualize the details of the most nourishing spot you can imagine.

(during those several more minutes the Being, having re-leased the pressure of many old, crusty thoughts and feelings from past experiences with people, situations, and items, realizes Its readiness to work with Its members in this process of unfoldment . . . .)

The Being: *(addressing Foot)* Well, head honcho, what do you think? Was it worth a half-hour-or-so change in your program?

Foot: *(with respectful relief and appreciation)* Please accept my apology for being so short with you. I forgot how tired I've been just getting the conference ready. I too, wish to thank you for lightening my load. I can now put a spring back into my Being's walk.

The Being: *(also feeling gratitude)* I'm glad I could help. *(eagerly)* And now I hope you can help me. I need to find out exactly what gets stored in all areas of the Physical body, because my own members are out-of-sorts. *(tentatively)* Do you suppose this would be a good time to hear from someone in that field? I know this will again change your carefully organized pro-gram, and you were so flexible as to shift things once al-ready . . .

Foot: *(with good-natured resignation)* No problem. Given your assistance, I would say that now is the perfect time for that kind of discussion, only I don't have my notes in front of me to know whom, if anyone, I can call up to the podium. But again, thank you for defusing this potentially disastrous com-motion.

(turning to the audience to speak as the Being rejoins Its members)

May I have your attention please. It seems our symposium this year has a mind of its own, . . .

(spontaneous laughter)

. . . and going along with this new flow, I would now like to announce yet another change in the program to allow for a guest speaker to talk specifically about the issues and items that store in different human body parts and areas, . . .

(Foot falters slightly, realizing that it is about to put—royally—its foot in its mouth, as it really doesn't know exactly how to continue at this point, or whether anyone present actually has the expertise to respond—or how to locate such a speaker on such short notice amongst the assembly. Suddenly, a flurry of activity breaks out at the side of the stage, and the stage manager, a Right Hand, rushes up to the podium and whispers excitedly to Foot.)

(even more befundled) Er, uh, it seems as if our guest speaker has just arrived. . . . *(quickly recovering its composure despite itself)* . . . And if our guest will please come on up to the podium—let's give a hearty round of applause for . . . .

(hearty cheering and applause erupts from the enthusiastic crowd)

Jaguar: *(to its compatriots)* I didn't catch the name. Did you, Wizard?

Wizard: *(mildly irritated)* Not me, the noise was too loud! How about you, Being, did you hear it?

The Being: *(quite thrilled at the turn of events)* No, I didn't catch the name either, but it looks like an authority figure, don't you agree?

Wizard: *(testily)* Hard to say. I'm more interested in what information is given, anyway.

(the lights dim as the mysterious guest speaker reaches the podium amidst thunderous applause . . . .)

In every job that must be done, there is an element of fun;
You find the fun and snap!—the job's a game;
And every task you undertake
Becomes a piece of cake
A lark! A spree! It's very clear to see!

—Mary Poppins*

Verily the lust for comfort murders the passion of the soul
and then walks grinning in the funeral.

—Kahlil Gibran, *The Prophet*

♡ CHAPTER THREE ♡

THE ASTRAL BODY THERAPIST

(From the audience, the guest speaker appears as a lumines-
cent light with no truly distinct characteristics. It seems to be
of medium height, with soft features and a full head of hair,
but lacking emphasis toward male or female attributes as far
as the Being can tell.)

Guest Speaker: *(accepting the podium from Foot)* Thank you . . . thank
you all. Technically speaking, I'm known as an Astral Body
Therapist, but please, you can call me Astro for short.

(polite applause)

*from Richard M. Sherman and Robert B. Sherman, "A Spoonful of Sugar," Walt Disney's Mary Poppins, © 1963 by Wonderland Music Co., Inc.

Astro: *(moving immediately into the substance of its presentation)* Thank you. In my experience . . . I've learned over the years that there is much more to each of you body parts than nerves, muscles, and bones. And, as we all know, not a one of you works alone: for you to function, you must be attached and in communication with all of the body parts that make a human Being. But before we go into specifics, I'd like to share with you my friends Harry and Frank. "Frank" is the personality I give to my Mental nature, which lives in the right side of my body. To balance things, I call my left side, where my Emotional holdings are located, "Harry." Here's an example of how Harry and Frank interact:

"*Sob . . . sob,*" Harry emotes.

"What's the matter?" Frank asks.

"I just can't take being ignored any more. I feel useless, and it's all so hopeless," Harry sighs.

"But Harry, I don't understand what brought all of this on. You are so quiet most of the time," Frank returns.

"Of course I'm quiet. Why bother, when you don't listen to me or consider my input of any importance," Harry retorts.

"Well, if that's how you feel, why the crying now?" Frank wonders.

"Because I can't live that way any more! I am designed to flow and release pressure within the Physical form. But every time I do, you override my sharing!" Harry hollers.

"Well, what do you expect of me when your outbursts are so unpredictable and embarrassing?" Frank shouts.

"There you go again, passing judgment on me when I am just trying to do my job!" Harry bellows. "Who put you in charge anyway?"

"Well, someone has to keep control of the situation!" Frank barks.

"Says who? I'm just as valuable around here as you are— even if I can't always state my case as eloquently as you do. Without a cleansing of feelings and built-up resentments, eventually the Physical form goes into dis-ease and can even cease to exist at all. Then where would you be, smarty pants?" Harry sneers.

"Well, all I'm trying to do is to protect the Being who lives inside this Physical form. But it doesn't look like you appreciate my efforts," Frank snaps.

"What I don't appreciate is not being included in your decisions. Have you ever noticed that our Being isn't particularly happy? Imprisoned maybe, in your style of safety, but not fully alive and excited about life or living!" Harry counters.

"To stay in control and not be hurt, sometimes you have to make sacrifices. You know that as well as I do," Frank retorts.

"Have you ever considered the possibility that I can *help* you in your endeavors, rather than always being dismissed?" Harry asks.

"Do you remember when the Being was five years old, and you completely fell apart on the first day of kindergarten, and all of the kids teased us unmercifully?" Frank recalls aloud with confidence. "At that time, the Being asked for *any way at all* not to have to deal with the other kids' teasing again, because it was too painful. Well, I offered to help, because protection is important to me, only I *have* to have complete control of things—or you would foul them up again."

"Listen to yourself! I know you live in the past and future, but that was over twenty-five years ago! Is it *remotely* possible that the Being feels differently now?" Harry points out sarcastically.

"I don't know," Frank answers stiffly. "I've never asked."

(Deer and Wizard gaze at each other in silence, each wondering if the other could possibly change . . . or if the other would even want to find out whether the Being's feelings have changed since the time they first passed out of full communication. . . .)

Astro: *(throwing it out to the audience)* Say, does this dialogue sound familiar to any of you Human Body Parts?

Various members of the audience: *(shouting)* Yes, yes . . . Oh yes! . . . So much so that it's become habit energy, routine! . . . Are you saying it doesn't have to be this way?

Astro: *(responding to the shouted question)* I believe so. As you can see, the Emotional nature, which occupies the left side of the body, has an entirely different view of things than its Mental counterpart on the right. And although corresponding body parts deal with the same issues, their vantage points can be entirely different—and that difference can become the deciding point between well-ness and ill-ness. I've discovered that the Being inside each human structuring has a three-part, integrated base system which includes its Mental and Emotional natures as well as its Physical attributes. In fact, the Emotional and the Mental systems are actually bodies in themselves that co-exist with you Physical Parts to produce well-ness moment by moment in our daily lives. It could be said that all decisions and basic human existence can be handled by one of these systems or a combination of the systems working together, but if one of the members or the integration of the systems is blocked, then the issues get stored in each of you as extra Physical weight to carry.

Also, even though the three members—Mental, Emotional, and Physical—together determine third dimensional living, it is you folks, as the Physical, who make up the densest of the three team players and ultimately have the final say in any matter. Otherwise stated, for all practical purposes, when the form goes, we go: we are no longer able to interpret ourselves as appearing separate from the whole and thereby to focus on only a portion of the whole. Therefore, when any of you Physical Body Parts finally get our attention with an ache or pain, it's really our *last* warning of an imbalance, not the first, and therefore requires our *full attention* to bring our perceptive aware-ness back on line, or as we would say, out of dis-ease or ill-ness, and back into well-ness!

So, in truth, it is the integration of these three densest bodies that produces the ideal operating basis of enthusiasm, hope, strength, and lack of pain. Does that answer your question?

(dead silence permeates the room . . . .)

Astro: *(confidently)* Well, hopefully all these perceptions will become clearer as we move along today. And with that notion in mind, I'd like to begin my in-depth discussion of specific body parts and regions with their correlating issues and items.

(with profound awe) Before I begin, I'd just like to say as a prelude that through my work with helping people to muster up to their own personal Magnificence, I've had the really great honor and pleasure of being with people in a way in which they are not often with themselves—and that is with *absolute* love and support. Then, lo and behold—by merging with another Being, and knowing that they are an Incredible, Magnificent, Priceless Gift, just by being in form—a true CONNECTION is made. I've been greatly and incredibly moved, at times to tears, through this merging process—of placing people on my massage table, of placing my hands upon their Physical forms, and of working through the Physical access points to reach the other two members of their base system, and in strengthening those other team players— because it really is a team effort, and, as in any team sport, one player can't do it all. The win comes for all of us when each of the base system members, full and complete, works together with the others for something greater than the individual parts, in this case human body parts.

(heads nodding in support of that notion abound throughout the auditorium)

(decisively) So, let's begin with the Feet—and not just because Foot happens to be our introducer today . . .

(snorts of laughter among the crowd)

. . . but because it's a good place to start. The Feet are like our scouts in life—just as in the covered wagon days, when the scouts would go out ahead to get an idea of the lay of the land

and to determine if any danger was eminent. In essence, the same is true for the Feet. They move out first and then bring the body along. They are lightweight, generally speaking, and therefore freedom of movement is critical to their taking us forward in life. The Toes act as a balance and help the body to realign with each new step, each step of growth and change in our life.

Specifically, the Left Foot reaches for adventure and the thrill of uncovering a new awareness. The Right one, on the other hand—or the other Foot in this case— . . .

(more snickers among a few boos)

. . . seeks out the unknown and strives to make it known to the rest of the body.

At this point I believe it would be helpful to have a word or two from a Foot. Perhaps our host today would like to make a comment—offer a personal point of view, so to speak.

Foot: *(flustered, taken a bit by surprise)* Well, I . . . okay. As I suppose you can tell, I am the Right Foot for my Being, and I'm so excited. Actually, it's because my Being is entering a new field of work that connects her computer background with child care. I don't fully understand it yet, but she seems to think it will really make a difference in the quality of life for young people whose parents must be away due to work commitments. It has been a bit hectic of late, as I have been focusing on this symposium. But now that I think of it, I've sort of been propelled along on her enthusiasm and the support of the Left Foot.

Astro: Thank you for sharing with us—and we'd like to thank you for all of your efforts to make this year's symposium possible.

(an immediate standing ovation resounds through the auditorium while Foot looks on with its feelings completely exposed)

(resuming its discourse) To continue, the Calf, or Lower Leg, deals with the future. As this is in the jurisdiction of the Mental nature, the Right Calf looks after the facts related to future endeavors. Perhaps a Being like the one you're attached to is preparing to move to another town. As we all know, there are simply hundreds of items that must be dealt with when moving to a new home. During these times, the Right Calf is weakened, and therefore any extreme exertion, such as long-distance running, could result in a sprained ankle or pulled ligaments. And, if this proposed move in any way affects your self-worth or financial security, even the Left Calf could be weakened.

You see, the *Left* Calf deals with the *Emotional* concerns of the future. As in the example before, a future event can either affect both calves or focus through one calf more specifically. For example, take the event of getting married. Besides the fact that there are plenty of plans to make, which by itself involves the Right Calf, the Being knows a major change is underway, with no guarantee that things will turn out as desired—an Emotional vulnerability which can impact the Left Calf. A major promotion at work or lack thereof can influence the Calf area as well.

So all issues involving *future value* of the Being or that bear any possibility of *pain in the future* will filter through the Left Calf. There is more and more awareness of abuse these days—and living in constant fear for one's life can put a severe strain on both Calves.

Also keep in mind that if one area of the body is in major upset, the signal gets sent throughout the body, and other areas naturally try to help out. So, a pain in the Back can be activated by an issue in the Right Knee, which is why human Beings are sometimes at a loss to understand the Physical signal they get!

(a Left Calf waves itself frantically to get recognized in the back of the auditorium . . . .)

Astro: *(alertly, with a smile of acknowledgment)* It seems we have a Calf who has something to say.

Left Calf: *(in a gush of pent-up frustration)* Boy, do I! For years people have been on my Being's case to get ahead, to make something of himself (my Being is a guy), to quit fooling around, and to get down to business in life. I mean, he's a wreck! He really does want to please his family, but he feels so dead when he starts an eight-to-five job. And then, before long, he's either been fired or quit. In any event, everyone gets disappointed, especially his dad, who keeps stressing that he is a self-made man. Well, bully for him!

All my Being gets is the stress—but no support to grow in his own way. You might say my Being is a dreamer. He sees visions of life as being beautiful and harmonious, and he dislikes discord, which his father thrives in. He wants to do something to capture the beauty in life, perhaps work outdoors as a forest ranger, but his dad keeps harping about getting a real job. I can hardly stand it any more, and I get pretty scared.

Astro: *(sympathetically)* I'm sorry to hear of your fear, Calf, and at the same time I'm grateful you feel safe enough to share your concerns with all of us. How do you feel right now?

Left Calf: *(pausing to take inventory)* . . . Well, I hadn't realized all of the panic I had been storing. . . . I know the facts haven't changed, but just now it doesn't seem quite so impossible to deal with as it had earlier.

(. . . *A hearty round of applause erupts in the huge room. As the noise dies down Astro again thanks this Body Part for sharing its experience.* . .)

Astro: Thank you, again, Left Calf. And now, to continue with the roster of Body Parts. . . . The Knees (and the Elbows, too) act as guards to our inner sanctuary and our particular point of view. After all, the future stuff has yet to occur, and all past stuff is very closely guarded by most folks. So, it's not surprising that all future items locate outside the inner sanctuary, from the Knee down. The Right Knee focuses on protecting the Self. It is constantly looking out for any comment or action that indicates that the Self might be judged or criticized. Then, at the first sense of such a perception, BAM!— the Knee closes its gate, isolating the Being from any future input. Have you ever talked to someone and had them discount what you said before they even really heard it? I've heard of a phrase that refers to someone as being "closed-minded." Well, I'll bet that the person in question hasn't a clue that that particular way of holding or viewing life sends a signal to the Right Knee to be on guard!

Bear in mind the important and plain fact that our individual Mental natures are all "other-directed." In other words, the Mental nature gets all of its perceived information from outside sources, which it then brings in through its "filters"— its understanding of the words it hears and how it holds those words as either "good" or "bad." So what it gets *isn't necessarily what actually happened* or *the truth!* But then again, how else could it accomplish its job of protecting the Self, unless it has total control over a particular situation?

Wizard: *(to itself, feeling confirmed)* That's always been obvious to me in terms of what's needed and best for the Being.

Deer: *(under its breath, having overheard Wizard's remark, and venturing a comment to defend its perception)* But isn't the point of living that we experience what life has to offer, not set up a narrow path that must be followed?

The Being: *(shushing them so they won't miss any of the information)...* Shhhh!—Please!

Astro: ...To continue with the Knees, the Left Knee, in particular, guards against infractions to one's Self-esteem. Since most of us have had our Emotional flow snared in some way, we all tend to be a little shaky in the area of Self-worth. In fact, it's very hard for us to grasp that *we do not have to prove our worthiness.* It just is, whether we are exuding it or not—or, otherwise stated, whether we do life right, wrong, upside-down, or backwards. The truth is that our Incredible, Magnificent, Priceless nature IS A GIVEN. This is why human Beings feel better when they go within, through meditation or quiet time with themselves.

(after a slight pause to allow the information to be received) Moving up to the Thighs, which contain our strongest set of muscles, we find that, not surprisingly, they hold our past. So, let me just ask you Thighs out there—if your Being had kept every piece of clothing they had ever worn on this planet since arriving as a baby, would that make much sense to you or to any of you other Body Parts?

(muted chuckles are heard throughout the auditorium. . . .)

After all, we grow and change, right? Well, think of ALL of your Being's life experiences and see them ALL stored in the Thighs (with the overflow in the Buttocks area). Tell me you haven't noticed that this particular Body Part is often much larger than just about any other!

(Murmurs of recognition ripple through the audience.)

However, unlike our clothes closets, which we continually update and clear out, our internal closets get more and more jammed up and packed in, so much that sometimes the Being simply can't afford to add one new item to their thoughts, feelings, or physical activity, or to retrieve a particular memory!

As you probably have already guessed, the Right Thigh is packed with all the details of living, while the Left Thigh holds on to all the upsets and incongruent feelings, interspersed with moments of joy and delight. The trouble is, how does one retrieve the items one wants to remember without uncovering a whole bunch of experiences it would rather forget? Or, more accurately put, how does one get the energy that is stuck in the Left or Right Thigh moving again? Well, the vocalizing exercise that the Being helped us with was definitely a step towards that end. A full answer to that question, my friends, is perhaps better left for a future workshop . . .

Audience: *(loud shouts and cries can be heard)* No! No! We want to know NOW!

Astro: *(with a broad smile, finding infinite humor in the situation)* Okay, okay . . . I see this conference truly does have a mind of its own. Perhaps we can address additional ways to move stuck energy, not only from the thigh area, but also anywhere in the body . . .

Several Thighs seated in the front rows: (hollering) Wait a minute! Don't we get a chance to share?

Astro: (quick to respond) Of course. However, considering the bulk of items you likely are sitting on, . . .

(muffled snickers in the auditorium)

. . . please bear in mind that we have only a one-day symposium, and there *are* other items on the agenda . . .

(The speaker glances over at Foot, who nods itself emphatically YES!)

. . . not to mention the additional information on moving stuck energy that everyone has indicated they are eager to hear . . .

Audience: (cheers and whoops)

A Right Thigh: (bellowing emphatically) Well, if you ask me, we carry some really important information concerning the growth of our Being. I'm not discounting the value of every Body Part; however, when we are jammed, it seems like every part gets affected in some way, because the past seems to dictate much of our present and seems to affect our future as well! Can you tell us why past experience and thought should carry so much weight for the human Being?

Astro: (frankly) That's a very good question, Right Thigh. I wish I had the answer to that one—and that it were so simple. No one intends to get caught up in confusion or frustration or fear, yet we have all run into that Being who complains of the same thing over and over again. Recognize that it takes a great deal of energy to pull our past into our present and turn it into our future! For example, at age six a human Being happens to suffer being bitten by a dog. For years, the Being rigorously avoids all dogs, until finally the Being hasn't one nice thing to say about any dog, at any time, and always reacts nervously around them. This is a classic case of a Mental override to an Emotional issue—the item is left unresolved, so every dog this person sees sets this particular conversation in motion, and the belief system becomes stronger until anyone who doesn't control their dog the way this Being thinks it should be done becomes a bad person and the Being gets to feel even more isolated and separate. What the Mental nature doesn't realize is that all this protection also imprisons the Self.

The Mental body, by nature, likes both to create and to protect. Sometimes the two functions get intertwined to the point where a Being finds itself focusing only on creating protection. One way to keep undesired energy away from the body is to run feelings through the Mental body, which shows up as judgments, criticisms, and negative or limited statements. This quite common action of "going on the attack" keeps the Being isolated and separate, resulting many times in bitterness. Then, to solidify this vantage point, the Mental looks for situations or visual evidence to prove itself right! . . .

(Hearing this, Wizard nods in self-satisfaction, feeling perfectly justified in its own actions, internally commending itself for being such a clever and ingenious fellow, and seeing nothing "wrong" with this assessment of its activities.)

Astro: . . . This entire syndrome of the Mental nature overriding the Emotional, by the way, appears to be quite prevalent on the planet Earth at this time. Such strong determination to make the manifested world match an individual perception is certainly powerful enough to set that particular vibration or energy in motion. Thoughts, especially when as belief systems they eventually become habit energy, are just as impactful to human Beings as physical form, because we are all made up of energy, just vibrating at different rates. That is why, when you are around a negative person who is setting off "negative vibrations," you get upset more easily than otherwise. Or, when you are in the presence of someone who vibrates more positively than you experience yourself, you feel better. For example, have you ever found yourself caught up in someone's contagious laughter, even when you were feeling low?

(murmurs of understanding ripple through the assembly)

So, the Right Thigh is full of unresolved issues that it, at the time, decided was its job to protect the Being from having to deal with. However, when we rely on the moment to determine our actions, we must rely more on the Emotional body, which the Mental body continuously tells us embarrasses us. So to prevent our Selves from looking stupid, we use old, past information to determine our present and also to turn it into our future!

(Astro, after pausing a moment to catch its breath and to have a drink of water, continues . . .)

Meanwhile, the Left Thigh stores old hurts and upsets. Unfortunately for most humans, these areas are quite full and often bursting to over-flow, which they do into the Buttocks' area. Now you Buttocks here today are well aware of this dilemma. Some Beings rent a five-by-seven-foot storage area (i.e., Buttocks), whereas others go for a twelve-by-twenty-four-foot space, and in all cases the area is filled to overflowing with the past items of the Thighs, making it difficult to do your own jobs.

(shouts of "Hear, Hear !" resound from the many Buttocks present)

A Buttocks from the middle of the audience: *(bellowing)* I beg your pardon! Just who do you think you are?

(a hushed stillness fills the auditorium)

Buttocks: *(absolutely furious)* Before you go making any more comments about my size, I'd like to inform you that I am *sick and tired* of being held as the blunt of your levity! I take my job of storage seriously, and if my Being really wanted to get rid of some of the old thoughts and feelings and issues it's carrying, it would tell me directly. Perhaps my Being *wants* to remember, so as to prevent these things from happening again—or to recall a wonderful experience. You have no idea what is important to me and my Being!

Astro: *(somewhat surprised at this explosive outburst, and realizing that a miscue has occurred)* Whoa . . . you are absolutely right, Buttocks. It is not my desire or intent to place my beliefs onto you. I'm sure you Body Parts are all fed up with that approach. Please forgive me for being so insensitive . . . . In all sincerity, I'm speaking to the general nature of things, with which many of us can identify, but there will always be those whose experiences do not apply or who cannot relate to these common occurrences. So, please accept my apology for making it sound as though you all must have had the same experiences. Perhaps, as I continue, the data will seem less intrusive.

Buttocks: *(feeling good for having spoken up for itself and for being heard, and in fact seeming more at ease and less tight than before it spoke)* Apology accepted.

(whispering aside to its immediate neighbor, another Buttocks)

Perhaps there is something to this releasing business. Maybe I'll pay closer attention to the rest of this part of the program.

Astro: *(after a brief pause to note that the Buttocks has indeed settled more comfortably into its seat)* So, besides bearing the overflow from the Thigh area, the Buttocks have their own domain of items to deal with. First of all, the gluteus medius muscle area on the right side responds to money issues— irregardless of whether you have a lot of money or few funds, all financial concerns register here. In addition, this area is responsible for repetitive thought. When you obsessively go over and over an issue in your mind, this area becomes weakened. These muscles are a part of the Lower Back system. So, you can begin to see how stressful thinking can weaken a portion of the Back and may even result in Lower Back pain.

On the left side, in the same area, just below the Hip, are issues of self-esteem and all close relationships. If the way one views one's Self or another is out of line with one's integrity or standards, then this area goes at odds with itself— and it cannot provide the physical support needed by the Lower Back. Not surprisingly, Lower Back pain is so prevalent now that it is practically accepted as *normal* in human Beings—but I dare say it is not *natural*.

(the speaker pauses briefly)

Wizard: *(taking advantage of the pause and whispering to the Being)* What's the difference?

The Being: *(wondering the same thing)* I don't know, exactly. Perhaps we can get an explanation.

(the Being raises Its hand to be called upon)

Astro: *(responding immediately)* Yes. . . . Do you—Being—have a question?

The Being: *(in somewhat of a quandary)* Well, we . . . I mean, my members and I are a bit confused about the meanings of "normal" and "natural." Aren't they one and the same?

Astro: *(truly enthused)* I'm so glad you noticed the use of terms. I sometimes have the idea that I'm speaking to myself at these lectures.

(a few chuckles are heard throughout the auditorium)

To answer your question—no, they are not the same. In fact, they are quite different. *Natural*, as it implies, flows with nature. It is always aligned—in balance and harmony with its surroundings—one with, inherent. In body form, we call it well-ness. *Normal*, on the other hand, refers to something that is typical, usual, but not true across the board. *Normal* is so prevalent that it just *appears* to be what's so. For example, a headache is normal because lots of human Beings get them, but a headache is not natural, because not everyone has them. A nose is natural, not only because everyone has one, but because even though some people break their nose or lose the ability to breathe through it, it is always designed for breathing. I hope this answers your question.

Being: *(relieved to know the distinction)* Yes, thank you!

(however, as the Being deftly notes out of the corner of Its eye, Wizard now sits a little lower in its chair—as though it is not quite as sure about things as it had thought it was)

Astro: *(moving along now)* Also in the Buttocks area, along the Spine and in connection with the Sciatic Nerve, are the issues of fear and stark terror. On the right side in this area, all of our unknowns kick-in—those aware-nesses which indicate to the Mental nature that things are out of control, which is where fear originates.

Now by the very nature of unknowns, control is not certain, but the Mental nature sometimes hates to think it is tied or connected to the Physical form. And then, in its own upset, it attempts to override the Emotional and Physical bodies. For all of you Sciatic Nerves out there, I don't need to tell you how painful it can be when you grip from the Mid-to-Lower Back, all the way down the Leg.

(murmurs of "Boy, is that the truth!" are heard throughout the auditorium)

Astro: *(pressing on with its point)* The Left side of the Buttocks, along the Spine, is equally infused with unbased fears and does not need the Sciatic Nerve to remind it of pent-up concerns and worries. For, at the first sign of upset, it is like a dam with huge holes in it, as all the built up anxious-ness and terror gushes out, uncontrollably, until some balance is regained. All in all, it's not a pretty sight from either the Mental or Emotional standpoint. So, not surprisingly in such cases, at the point where survival is perceived to be the issue, the two natures, Mental and Emotional, tend to merge to escape incredible pain or the possibility thereof. This is not unlike human Beings when they are caught in disaster—

whether by human hands or nature's—and end up bonding together, setting all differences aside . . . only as far as I can tell, the effect hasn't been a lasting one as of yet.

(Astro pauses briefly for effect)

But, then, who knows, perhaps Beings are beginning to recognize their connected-ness.

The Being: *(aside, to Itself)* I wonder if the speaker is referring to me?

Astro: *(slyly)* In any event, having acknowledged the issues that get SIT-uated in the Buttocks . . .

(boos and groans from the crowd, including some good-natured guffaws from the assemblage of Buttocks, who have become noticeably more relaxed)

. . . we now move to the Back in general and then the Lower, Middle, and Upper Back sections. But first, does anyone need a bathroom break? I do get carried away and tend to forget that there are some Bladders here today.

(mass laughter and several more groans . . .)

Let's take a thirty-minute break. *(Astro suddenly recalls that the question of how to move stuck energy had gone unanswered . . .)* When we get back, with our chair-Foot's permission, we'll see if we can't come back to some additional ways for clearing the issues that have become unconsciously and unduly stuck in any part of the body, and then continue with the rest of the Body Parts.

(Foot nods its approval, while the members of the assembly applaud, then rise and move en masse into the aisles as they exit for the break)

Wizard: *(to its companions, pompously calling attention to itself, but ironically without grasping that it, Wizard, is also here to shift its perceptions)* See, now wasn't I right—as usual? Aren't we getting exactly what we came to get?

Every time a factor is rendered irrelevant,
it is a form of judgment and denial. Reality is not
something that should be delineated and defined
in such a limiting way. Reality is supposed to be fluid
and evolving. Everything has consciousness,
and nothing can be denied its role in creation.

—from *The Right Use of Will*

♡ CHAPTER FOUR ♡

THE QUEST CONTINUES

The Being: *(turning to Jaguar)* So, what do you think, Jaguar? Were you aware of all of these cross-currents going through you, carrying thoughts, issues, and feelings?

Jaguar: *(rather amazed)* Actually, I never quite understood the process. I just react when the pressure to my parts is more than I can handle. I guess you could say I never really viewed things from any other direction, especially yours. . . . I mean, I've always been aware of impacting thoughts and feelings and reacted accordingly. But it never dawned on me that I was more than a vessel or a place for other items to come through. I now see that I have lots more to contribute to your development than just as a storage unit. And, now I feel it's even more important to me to see that the Mental and Emotional team players continue to participate together and not attempt to operate solely on their own.

The Being: *(glowing)* Thanks, Jaguar. It is such a joy to know that I have your full support!

Wizard: *(rudely interrupting)* Well, I try hard to help, too! It's not easy to figure things out in advance to spare you some grief. *(Wizard's voice rises to a bellow)* And what about all of those times I've saved you from embarrassing situations? That takes energy, you know!

The Being: *(sensing Wizard's growing hurt and indignation)* Slow down, Wizard; you are going to blow a fuse. Just because I am beginning to align with my Physical body representative doesn't mean I appreciate you any less.

If I have taken you for granted at any time, please forgive me. I'm just learning about all of you, as you are learning about me. Quite frankly, I wasn't even aware of you as a team to assist me here in third dimensional form on planet Earth, until just now. So please relax and free up your thoughts, so you can get as much out of this lecture as possible. I have an idea that it will take *all* of us hearing this data to be able to integrate it later.

(Wizard contemplates the Being's words and decides to let down its guard, on the off chance that something valuable might be said)

The Being: *(turning to Deer)* How about you, Deer? What do you think about the lecture so far?

Deer: *(rather sheepishly)* There seems to be so much to learn. I admit that I am a bit overwhelmed. It's like opening up a wound to clean it so it will heal faster, but it hurts to do so. I have been afraid for so long that I'm not sure I can imagine being unafraid. I know it sounds silly, but . . .well, the fear is familiar to me and, in an odd way, I've developed particular responses to the fears that are habitual to me—and therefore they haven't required much of my attention. I guess you could say I haven't been very available to you, but rather more concerned with my own comfort, and now that I realize that, it makes me sad.

I don't even know where I got the idea to pull in my awareness and operate out of such a tiny area. But what I've witnessed so far today has shown me just how small I've become. It's no wonder Wizard doesn't want to have much to do with me. I haven't offered much lately in the way of assistance to either of you, let alone the Physical form.

The Being: *(pondering the depth of Deer's dilemma)* That's quite an insight, Deer. . . and it carries a great deal of wisdom for us all.

(Jaguar and Wizard mutely nod their heads in affirmation, and the foursome sits in silence until the break is over, when, with the audience reassembled in the auditorium, Astro returns to the podium)

Astro: *(catching up to itself)* First of all, I must apologize, for I had totally forgotten about giving you the information on ways to relieve built-up pressure or stuck energy inside the systems. You see, I have what I affectionately term "Sometimer's Disease"—sometimes I remember, and sometimes I don't.

(polite murmurings of understanding and chuckles of appreciation throughout the audience)

Astro: *(getting back to the question at hand)* I'd like to say at the outset that both the Mental and the Emotional bodies will benefit from these techniques. One way to release pent-up anger is to write a long letter to the person involved, then read it—out loud if circumstances allow it, since vocalizing helps move energy up and out of the Physical system, and using dramatic emphasis if possible (i.e., shouting as though the person were in the room). Then tear up the letter and burn it.

Another means is to close your eyes and see yourself and this other person in the situation that did not go "according to Hoyle." At this point, give yourself permission to rearrange the circumstances to your liking in your mind's eye, and talk or act out the revised scenario in a life-like manner.

Another method is to vocalize while alone in the car, with windows rolled up, so as not to involve others. Feel free to sing loudly to music, roar like a lion, shout profanities, and just in general make a silly nuisance of yourself, until laughter rules the moment.

Also, if you liked the amphitheater process that the Being so graciously led us through earlier today, then by all means make use of the stage and the twenty-five-foot-tall speakers with any and all situations, people, or items that are as yet unresolved within you. Be sure to speak to these energies directly, and follow that by dissolving everything on the stage and the stage itself, then planting, in your virgin soil, that which works for and supports you.

Physically speaking, you could take a brisk walk or engage in a strenuous workout until the feelings and thoughts become stabilized.

Vocalizing in any of these scenarios is effective because sound provides power to move blocked Emotional energy, open the gates located at all the joints, and provide the *oomph!* to move both thought and feeling up and out of the Physical form. It also lifts the spirit, allowing for greater awareness of yourself and the environment around you.

Using the Breath also helps, since people who are operating with a lot of control issues tend to experience hypertension and and don't always breathe very deeply. Quite often control issues can be disguised as sadness or depression, since these operate as a control to literally "sit on" a Being's anger, because anger itself motivates us to action.

Also, sitting in a warm bath dosed with apple cider vinegar at the end of the day has great drawing power—the cider vinegar draws off feelings of "I don't want to," or "I don't feel like it," and pulls the guards off duty—the Knees, Ankles, Elbows, etc.—allowing more pliability and openness, so the systems can generate acceptance, balance, and well-ness more quickly. Then, while sleeping, the members can more quickly align. In the morning, even though your circumstances haven't changed overnight, chances are you'll feel better about them.

(as an afterthought) Also, when allowed to leave the Physical body, thoughts are released outward through the Wrists and Ankles, and feelings through the Pores of the Skin—we wish to acknowledge those Body Parts for their important contributions—

(appreciative cheers ring out)

So, all these physical activities—walking, vocalizing, writing, trembling, laughing, crying, and so on—help thoughts and feelings move through more freely, freeing up you, the Being, to be more present in the moment—with the full realm of possibilities in the Mental field, and pure enthusiasm in

Emotional expression not trapped and caught—and allowing expansion and fluidity in the moment.

Does that help—am I being specific enough?

Foot: *(responding for the group)* Thank you so much for those particular examples. I, for one, will encourage my Being to practice one or more of them, starting tomorrow!

(enthusiastic shouts of approval and gratitude rock the rafters)

(Astro simply beams, thrilled to have made a difference, while waiting for the energy to settle down . . .)

Astro: *(continuing in a strong voice)* And now, continuing with the issues held in the Back, as I was about to say before the break, not surprisingly, the entire Back deals with all issues of support. Once again, we can see the inter-relatedness of these issues on many levels. For example, physically, the Spinal Nerves, Muscles, and Bones all work together to get cross-communications to all Parts of the Body. Also, the Being, looking for support from Itself and others, strengthens or weakens Itself by Its relationship to each person. We first ran into specific issues of relationship in the Left Upper Hip area, and now we can look to the Back for how these issues appear to each of us—and this varies considerably to each Being, because each one has different lessons to learn—and both the relationships issues *and* the lessons are affected by the different natural talents each of us possess. So, you see, it's a complicated grid. Optimally, the back signifies, in its position of maximum support, each Being "getting" Its own pricelessness—YOU knowing that you need no one else to stand behind you to establish your value for YOU. In other words, it is remembering that the Universe is counting on You to do You. The Back truly represents your ability to stand in your own support of your own particular talents and for your own particular lessons while in this form, thereby opening up the possibility for others to support you, too. Quite frankly, we cannot give to others or receive from others that which we have yet to give ourselves.

(Astro pauses to allow the participants to ponder the enormity of the notion)

(the Being and Its members are deep in thoughtful silence)

Deer: *(thinking to itself)* I wonder what my own part might be in solidifying Wizard's point of view towards me—or just what aspect of my "Magnificence" I *haven't* shared—through withholding my *oomph!*—that Wizard could "back"?

Wizard: *(admitting to itself under its breath)* I guess it's true that I certainly have been backing my own point of view but not that of any of the other members. . . .

Astro: *(moving ahead)* Now, since I've brought it up, allow me to speak to the issue of natural talents here. People I've spoken to keep asking, "What is my purpose?" and so on, and I say it all relates to your natural talents. We are each a piece of a huge jigsaw puzzle, and each of us has a particular contribution to make to the puzzle as a whole—one that is natural to us as an individual point of awareness and also critical to the overall, collective program. Yet, many people have had their talents ignored or criticized, and this has resulted in the loss of the Beings' conscious awareness of these natural expressions of individual Self. In fact, when people point out a natural talent to someone, the talent usually seems so natural to the

Being that It considers the talent to be no big deal—and It may even have overlooked the talent completely in Its search for purpose.

What kinds of talents are out there? For example, one person greatly attunes to animals, and they easily see their part in the whole picture of life. Another person can physically look at some nuts and bolts and easily create a motor. Someone else can talk to others in a way that enthuses everyone to join in a particular project. All of this relates to enjoying our work as well as interacting with others. So you see, to say in general that any particular item does (or does not) support humans, relates to no one—it just doesn't hold water. Or, when someone says, "For heaven's sake, just do such and so, and all will be well!" or makes a blanket statement such as, "Anyone who does that (whatever *that* is) couldn't possibly be supported!"—well, these types of statements have no reality in them. You might want to remind yourself here that whenever a human Being hears or delivers judgment, criticism, negativity, or limitation, the person's Mental nature is at that point overriding one of their other members—Emotional or Physical—if not both.

So, at the risk of repeating myself, the bottom line is that an individual's Back is in charge of support, but the support in question must be determined on an issue-by-issue basis in seeing whether a particular experience or piece of information is supportive to the Being or not. To go back to the image of the many spokes of a wheel—all are equally distant from the center or source, but each has a slightly different vantage point or perception. *All views* are not only valuable, but necessary for the wheel to move easily. As such, we all have the natural support and full backing of the universe for our particular point of view/lessons/talents.

As I often tell folks, I have no problem when someone has a point of view that might be different from mine. I don't even mind that they have a point of view about me. I only have a problem when that someone attempts to make me take on *their* point of view, discounting my own, and not supporting "me doing me."

(murmurs of agreement ripple through the crowd)

Wizard: *(whispering to the others)* Sounds kind of complicated to me.

Deer: *(venturing an opinion)* Not really. In any given moment, the truth is most evident.

(Jaguar and the Being notice that Deer's voice sounds stronger than usual)

Astro: *(from a place of personal experience)* Unfortunately, when someone else attempts to superimpose their point of view, often we feel acutely the misperception of being *unsupported*, when our natural contributions or points of view are criticized, judged, negated, or limited in any way.

(as Astro pauses, Deer, Being, and Jaguar all direct their gaze pointedly at Wizard, who arches one eyebrow quizzically in response)

Returning to you specific Physical Body Parts, the Lower Back, being directly opposite the Intestinal Tract, where deep feelings are stored, is the support behind the Being's deeper feelings. I once heard of a little girl who desperately wanted to go to the grocery store with her mother. Who knows why this time was so important to her. In any event, her mother was in a hurry and said, "I'll be right back," and left her daughter at home. In later years, this young lady discovered she had a terrible abandonment issue, with lots of internal scars that had resulted in severe Lower Back pain. The doctors simply couldn't figure it out. They had given her wonderful Physical care, but the Back didn't let up until she uncovered this one occasion with her mother.

(ooohs and aaahs ripple throughout the auditorium . . .)

Astro: *(interjecting as the noise dies down)*

Amazing, isn't it! Now, a word of caution—bear in mind the spokes of a wheel once again—and that our different individual temperaments and lessons will result in different responses to the same set of stimuli. One person's abandonment issue that arose because they were left at home while their mom went to store, is another child's opportunity to be home alone. Each of us has an individual pace at which we grow and different criteria to work with, and it is up to each of us to discover this for ourselves.

Moving up to the Middle Back area, below the Shoulder Blades, this body region literally says, "Get off my back!" or "Get off my case!" People who feel ridden a lot, feeling pressure to perform a set way all of the time, for someone else's benefit, begin to carry their ensuing bitterness and resentment in this Middle Back area. I have found this to be true many times with the oldest child in the family, especially if there were several children to watch over. These folks are also often called upon to be an example, sometimes even to achieve what their parents hadn't achieved as children. This area also weakens for some people who strive continually for greater and greater achievement, never feeling they are fully okay at any point, or that any achievement is ever enough.

The Upper Back and Shoulder area carries two functions that sometimes seem contradictory in nature. From the Mental standpoint, this area contains responsibility. We've all known the very highly competent person, self-sufficient, not needing anyone, all-together, and so on. I'll be the first to admit that this type of strong energy carries me along at times. However, this same Upper Back and Shoulder area, from the Emotional angle, deals with maximum Emotional support. That's why hugs feel so-o-o-o-o good! I've noticed, though, that the very responsible Beings don't seem to get as much Emotional support as someone who is less sure of themselves. Now there's a quandary—for every Being has the ability to be strong and still enjoy the letting go and nurturing feeling of having someone else to lean on. Once again, you can easily see the seeds of bitterness and resentment growing inside a Being who is always accountable, along with the helplessness of someone who is considered less than they truly are.

Finally, the back of the Physical body also contains two Control Centers, and these are located on top of each Shoulder Blade. On the right side perches the Mental Control Button. What I mean by this is that the muscles on top of the Shoulder Blade house the generating point or headquarters of the Mental body's holding pattern. And, once pressed in on, this Control Center shoots impulses all the way up the Neck and through the occipital points to the Brain. When circumstances appear out of control or the Being feels in any way endangered, the Mental Control Center grips very tightly, causing the whole right side of the body to lock up. On the other hand, the Left Shoulder Blade keeps tabs on any and all occurrences that might be emotionally unnerving. For example, during wedding plans, when feelings are so prevalent and sensitivities are running high, the left muscles on top of the Left Shoulder Blade will be trigger-happy at the least provocation. And, in a split moment, these can jam up the Left Shoulder, Neck, and Head areas. This can also hold true for any item that involves personal worth and self-love or lack thereof.

A Neck: *(rising up to speak from the left side of the audience)* Can I talk? . . . Please, let me speak!

Astro: *(quick to shift its focus)* Yes, Neck, what would you like to share?

Neck: *(thrilled to be recognized)* I am so glad to hear someone relate the intricacies of my body part. Since I am basically a thoroughfare, whatever is going on in my Being's Shoulders affects me and my ability to remain strong, yet flexible. In addition, all of the thoughts that occur in her Brain can also block my freedom of movement. Talk about being the ham in the sandwich! Any help you can give me would be greatly appreciated.

Astro: *(with true compassion)* I will do my best—but first I want to speak about some internal organs and the part they play in this trilogy.

As I mentioned earlier, the Intestinal and Stomach areas house the Being's very deepest feelings and corresponding incidents. In fact, some such feelings have been packed in so tightly that the Being has almost forgotten they are there. Much of what stores here is not even on the conscious level— and for many, it is the most guarded area. In some cases, the

Being would literally rather *die* than have these feelings and memories surface!

The Being: *(shouting in outrage)* Wait a minute! I'm a Being, and I simply can't believe any Being would go to such extremes. After all, without a Physical form, a Being has no house to live in, no place to put Its experiences.

Astro: *(a bit startled by the intensity of the Being's outburst)* True enough. However, some thoughts and feelings appear to be too much for some human Beings to bear. It's not a rational decision to die from this cause. In fact, for some, it is a matter of survival.

The Being: *(realizing that It has much to be grateful for)* Well, I guess I can see how that might possibly take place. Suddenly I can really appreciate my own interest in living.

Astro: *(resuming with an air of command)* To continue, whereas the Stomach and Intestines house the deepest feelings and the incidents that triggered them, the Lung and Heart areas are most predominant in determining individual well-ness. It's not at all surprising that, when a Being is in survival mode or fear, the breath is very shallow—as though a full breath would expose them to the very thing they seek to avoid.

As for the Heart, there isn't a one of us who hasn't put our Self out there, only to have it denied, ignored, or outright attacked. Then the Heart recoils in protection, only to find itself separated from the very awareness it seeks. I've been told there are several techniques available to humans now, different types of body work and other therapies, to bring these incongruencies to the conscious level, where the Being can choose to change them or not. But for our purposes here today, it suffices for me to say that most Hearts, if viewed purely from the vantage point of energy flow, could stand to be recharged and flushed out—if indeed they are to last the duration of the Physical form. Any Hearts here today who would like to share?

Hearts: *(en masse in a thunderous roar and waving wildly for recognition by the speaker)* Yes, yes! Oh, yes! Here! Over here! I say! Yes!

Astro: *(feeling momentarily overwhelmed by this response)* Let me see....There are so many of you....Why don't we start at the back of the auditorium and work our way forward. I apologize in advance that we don't have the time to call on all of you. But . . . perhaps you can find it in your *Heart* to forgive me.

(soothing chuckles are heard, after which a Heart in the very back row begins to speak . . .)

A Heart: *(grateful for the opportunity to speak)* Most of all, I want to thank all of you for showing up here today. It warms me to think that conscious awareness is beginning to operate here as a connected whole. I've known all along that LOVE is all that is, and that all of us and our Beings will heal more quickly when a loving vibration is near. I'm so full of love and admiration, just sitting here, that I know my Being will feel better when I get home. Bless you all.

(A "hearty" round of applause breaks free as the Heart finishes speaking . . . .)

Astro: *(focusing on the crowd once again)* Okay, you over there to the left—towards the back . . . *(pointing)* . . . yes, you. What would you like to say?

Another Heart: *(raspingly, faintly, and with great effort)* Unlike the Heart who just spoke, I have been filled with such bitterness for so long that I feel old and tired. At first I tried to ease the pain of my Being, but by age eleven, the fire had been drowned out of him with physical abuse and emotional strangling—leaving me dry and brittle. My ability to regenerate and connect with the love vibration was severely damaged, and I have felt cold and dead ever since. Fortunately, or maybe not, I pump blood automatically—but it is without any life-giving force—just empty repetition. My Being is a male, old before his time, with no family or friends. He lives on the street, hoping the next moment will be his last, but not strong enough to end his life himself. I was only able to get here today with the help of a couple of Heart friends, but it simply may be too late for me.

(The room grows so quiet that the silence seems to have a voice of its own. Finally, after a long pause, a Left Knee speaks up.)

Left Knee: *(whispering kindly)* I have an idea of what you are feeling, Heart. I've been broken, smashed, relocated, and operated on—and I still hold the terror of being attacked again. It is so bad that my Being (a female) walks with a limp now. But thanks to the strength of *her* Heart, I am beginning to get my old enthusiasm back. She was told she'd never be able to walk on her Left Leg again, because of the damage done to me, but she refused to believe it. Now, after years of physical therapy and lots of family support, we get around. Oh, I know it won't be like before, when she was so active athletically, but we do have movement. And, I know that I for one am grateful for all of her Heart's support, and . . . well, I'm thinking that since you are a Heart, perhaps we other Body Parts can send you and the other Hearts here today the love and gratitude within us for all that you Hearts do for us. Believe me when I say that we would not be able to regenerate without you!

Astro: *(booming with enthusiasm)* That's a terrific idea! Let's all focus our attention on all of the Hearts in the room, but particularly this one—sending it love, compassion, and joy— and see if anything happens. Say, Foot, how about some inspiring music for this venture?

Foot: *(pondering)* Let me see. Ah, yes, I have the perfect tape . . . Just a moment now to set it up . . . *(momentary pause)* . . . Okay, here we go!

(For fifteen full minutes, the sounds of nature and running water fill the auditorium as all of the participants send their love and support out to all Hearts, but specifically to this one lone Heart.)

(Soon, visible energy currents appear to be flowing from throughout the auditorium toward that one Body Part, and the audience perceives that the Heart's energy is beginning to glow as though it were on fire. As the particular, lone Heart continues to ignite like a flame, the color of the Heart changes from a dull, dark, brownish-red to a bright red so brilliant that the arteries and veins connected to it become crystal clear with the richness of the blood being filtered. At that moment, each Body Part begins to disengage its awareness, allowing the recharging Heart to glow on its own.)

(Oooohs and ahhhs are heard throughout the room as the lone Heart continues to generate its own brightness, like the other Hearts in the room.)

Foot: *(in total awe)* Would you look at that! I'm not sure I would
            have believed it if I hadn't seen it for myself. What a miracle!

Astro: *(quite impressed)* Yes, indeed. It is truly a miracle that each of
            you participants today could get outside your own concerns
            long enough to make your energy available to another Body
            Part.

            And just think if it isn't true that all of you individual Body
            Parts—and Beings, too—have come to accept that, as your-
            selves, you have little impact on life. Yet, I dare say that today
            you have witnessed just how powerful you, as LOVE, are—
            for, you see, not a one of you is drained, as you might
            expect—but rather, together, you created a greater vibration,
            from which all of you benefitted.

            *(The audience, each reflecting on themselves, begins to see
            that indeed it is true . . . that the lone Heart is not the only
            glowing Body Part in the auditorium! A feeling of closeness,
            even vulnerability, becomes evident. . . .)*

Astro: *(pausing, as though to recover a thought)*. . . And, before I
            forget, *vulnerability* is found in three different parts of the
            body—between the Toes, the insides of the Thighs, and also
            the Chest area. This is why, when I work with a particular
            human Being, I begin by having them lie face down on the
            table, and I start at the Feet, both to gain access to the body
            members without touching into vulnerability issues, and to
            alleviate as much initial uncertainty as possible.

            For, once I enter the Being's energy field, it is my responsibil-
            ity to provide the space in which safety and trust can form as
            quickly as possible, so vulnerability will surface. To set this
            action in motion, I use the same order in working with a Being

as the order in which I have shared here today about the issues housed by all the specific Body Parts. In fact, I've discovered that each is a building block upon the others. So, in doing Astral Body Therapy, I also use verbal questions as an unimposing way to access that Being's members.

(reflecting on past experiences, Astro gazes out over the audience as though seeing into another dimension) Over the years I've noticed, in what I call my "mini-surveys," that there are many different perceptions to the same situation— and that which we call "right" for one person is inappropriate for another. The key to it all is acceptance—and that is not synonymous with understanding, but it does affect safety, which determines whether a Being will even consider vulnerability.

In truth, we are all learning that individual perception is what affects our notion of connected-ness or separation—or, otherwise stated, it is our individual perception as to whether we feel loved and supported in learning our life's lessons, and therefore free to be vulnerable and open, or whether we feel like we're an independent agent, operating completely in isolation, unable to count on anyone or anything—and often enough, not even ourselves, thereby closing off the bridge of connected-ness with others. Until this issue is settled on a planetary level, meaning that until everyone feels fully loved and supported within, then we as Beings feel we must be "on guard," protecting our weak points, and putting forth tremendous effort to counterbalance all the energies we encounter from which we appear to be isolated. These appear to us as huge dichotomies: with crime on the increase, we feel we must counter with more police protection. With drug dealers on the loose, we attempt to balance this energy with more

Don't-Do-Drugs campaigns. With car-jackers increasingly prevalent, we develop new ways to protect our vehicles—and so on.

All of these are external examples, but there are internal dichotomies that we trap ourselves with, as well. For all of the negative thoughts that we have collectively generated, we balance with literature on good deeds and forgiveness. For all the withheld, unstated, unvoiced hurts and abuse we sustain, we strive for individual aid to find the safety to release. For all the Physical forms that are not exercised and cared for, we offer fun, easy ways to motivate the Being to get the Physical body in motion, through sports and all forms of movement and nourishment.

However, by protecting the vulnerable side of ourselves, we end up imprisoning the Being within and cutting ties with outside phenomena. Whenever the Self is withdrawn or withheld, it contributes to the appearance or illusion of great separation.

Like I said, if the opposing counterpart to any one energy did not exist, we would literally lose the belief system we've all agreed to that keeps the delicate balance of gravity that we are accustomed to, and we would all fall off the Earth into space.

(a shout rings out from the audience, drowning out Astro's voice)

Shouter: *(loudly and indignantly)* Wait just a minute! Are you actually saying that these dichotomies or balancing opposites actually create the gravity of our environment?

(other snorts of disbelief are heard . . .)

Astro: *(smiling in knowing way)* Well, let me answer the question this way: more aptly put, it is our collective belief system that provides us with a means to interact on the planet, via gravity, and it would be terribly inconvenient if we lost that belief by discounting dichotomies, thereby dropping off the planet because we have no means like gravity to secure our footing. The nature of gravity is that it is the only item that we, as human Beings, can count on in our physical reality to always be in operation: it never doesn't function. In other words, if you go to jump out the window, gravity doesn't care if you are wealthy or not, or how well-liked you are, you will go SPLAT! like anyone else. So, gravity is the physical result of all these energetic dichotomies—as far in one direction as crime goes, we respond with an equal amount of energy put towards police intervention. To the degree that some children go without an adequate education, we attempt to reach as many of these children as possible with outreach programs.

The bottom line is, if there were no *resistance* to some particular thing or idea, that issue would disappear from the planet. So, like I said, if the physical counterpart to any particular energy did not exist, we would literally lose the means to engage in life in human form, on the earth, because gravity wouldn't exist, and we, in turn, would literally "lose it" and fall off the earth into space.

(several chuckles are heard throughout the audience)

You may laugh, but in the arena of vibration and pure energy, I wouldn't be surprised if there was some validity here—even though the notion is "just a little" farfetched.

(a wave of murmured "you've-got-to-be-kidding!" comments continues to ripple through the audience at the idea presented)

The good news is, we don't have to go to such extremes to maintain this balance within the nature of dichotomies, for within each of us lies the means to hold the notion of duality as a whole, in which case the need to go to such extremes becomes unnecessary.

Astro: *(waiting for the shock to wear off and maintaining its Chesire-cat-like expression)* Fortunately, we do not have to test gravity, because we as Beings live our whole life in a world *full of* dichotomies. It is a known fact that these bodies are made to go the distance, so the evidence that many humans are having "technical difficulties" mildly suggests that some vantage points are at-a-tilt. And, as all of life is made up of dichotomies, the further off-line we get about Being-ness and physically being here on planet Earth, the further away our goals of Peace, Joy, Love, and Support get from day-to-day living.

I know this idea seems so "heavy" or "far out," but let me bring it closer to home. If you close your eyes, the world as we see it disappears. Therefore, all interpretation of outside influences disappear, and we are left with our "Self," which is synchronized with the larger view of life. Yet, inside our own body, each of us has the ability to create our next, external image any way we want. At first it might seem like just a nice idea, but in a relatively short time, about four to six weeks, that idea moves into our modus operandi, and shows up in the world we see at large. So, all that I see in the world is but a reflection of how I am holding my relationship to myself, or a specific person, via the world at large.

It's a matter of training, with lots of habit energy to pass through. For example, have you noticed that when you start a new exercise program, at first you have to "think about" doing it, and sometimes you even forget to do it, or have to drag yourself to the venture? Depending on your natural inclinations, it might take you one to two months before the Physical form sends you signals of looking forward to the event. By then, it takes lots less thought and becomes habitual. Remember, those habits we like, we call "good," and those habits we don't like, we call "bad."

Astro: (as if waking from a trance) Boy, I guess I sort of went off on a tangent, didn't I?—I *am* aware that sometimes we flap our lips for our own benefit more so than for others'. This feels like one of those times! Any questions?

(mass silence)

(during the silence, Wizard muses to itself that much of what Astro alluded to was a long way off from reality on this planet, and thinks, "I just wonder where Astro is from . . . REALLY . . . ?")

Astro: (fully back to the moment of now) Okay, before I move on to the Head and Neck areas, I'd like to include the Arms, which again, like the Legs, have both a Mental and an Emotional vantage point. Starting with the Hands—like the Feet, we know them to be road maps of the entire human Physical body. They also enable human Beings to "grab hold" of a physical object or an idea that is ready to take form. The Hands literally grip the possibilities of life and enable a Being to pull itself out of a rut. The Right Hand keeps track of what has been worthy to keep, while at the same time it reaches for what is yet to be. On the other *hand*, . . . (the speaker pauses in an obvious manner) . . .

(the audience responds with stifled chuckles)

. . . the Left Hand exudes the warmth and depth of feelings about these memories and dreams. Together, a balance is reached, just as a rock climber ascends, and then realigns before ascending again—keeping a hold on value, and deeply feeling one's accomplishments and goals.

Advancing to the Forearm, we move into the storage area of frustration—all of those little items that in themselves are just bothersome, but when built upon each other, become over- whelming. When this happens, they enter the inner sanctuary through the Elbows. At this point, the human Being is known to get quite agitated and send stress levels soaring. On the Right Arm, the build up has a lot of "what ifs . . ." attached to it, which accelerates into fears—always of the unknown— while the Left side has tiny worries and concerns that affect personal worth or lack thereof. Quite often this build up in one or both sides has the effect of shutting down the Lymph system, which is designed to handle all non-natural items in the body.

(several Hands start waving . . .)

Astro: *(quick to respond to a member of the audience)* Yes . . . what is your question—you there, in the ninth row.

A Hand: *(with curiosity piqued)* What do you mean by non-natural items? I mean, isn't everything part of nature?

Astro: *(glad to see that the participants are interacting with the information)* Right you are. I knew what *I* meant by what I said, but you can see how easy it is to misconstrue things. Here, I was referring to smog and airborne chemicals, artifi- cial additives and preservatives, smoke, exhaust, and food colorings. And thank you for asking the question. It's so important to get clarification *whenever* you are unsure of a statement or action. Otherwise, uncertainty and doubt creep in, and many times judgment jumps in if, in lack of understanding, you find yourself embarrassed or made fun of. Besides, when we don't clear up these "loose ends" and "complete," at least up to the present moment, we are left carrying these embarrassments, misperceptions, and add to our at-a-tilt-ness, so the next time we encounter each other, we are ill at ease, and *full* Self-expression is not possible.

(Astro takes a moment to gather its thoughts while sipping some water)

To continue about the Upper Arm, once these frustrations build up and move past the Elbow guards, they are treated by the Being as a major upset—and all of the Joints, like gates, close, and the Physical form is no longer able to fully access itself.

This gate-like quality of the Joints have a real impact on the three dense bodies' communications system, which all contribute their different responses to any given situation that has built up into an upset. To get a picture of the Mental body's point of view, imagine visually looking into an ocean where the tip of an iceberg has been severed: the Mental body might say all is well, even though the iceberg still exists under the water out of view. In terms of the Physical body, the Back may be dealing successfully with support issues, but it can't get that information to an injured Leg if the energy flow is blocked at the Joints. And, even though the Emotional and Physical bodies are both in the moment and communicate directly, if an extreme amount of hurt enters the Physical form as a result of, say, a broken engagement, the Joints, like gates, will close off the areas around the Heart—so as to prevent the pain from flowing to other areas of the body. Again, then, on the Mental level—which occurs quite often—the Being might even deny there is an issue at all. Once this occurs, any sense of connected-ness as human Beings goes right out the window, and often is replaced with survival techniques, where the individual's experience becomes the only consideration. As we withdraw our thoughts and feelings from our loved ones, all involved can feel the severing of that connected-ness we all seek, which shows up as loss of Love.

The Upper Arm is like a bridge between the buildup of tiny frustrations and the major areas of trust and flexibility, which lodge in the Neck. It is the duty of the Upper Arm to act as a buffer against these built-up frustrations so that they are not able to reach the Neck area and therefore become a major concern. Unfortunately, many human Beings don't pay attention to these warnings, and before long, the Neck—usually a main thoroughfare—is all jammed up, severely constricting the incoming energy to the Head, as well as outgoing thoughts. So, its ability to deal with trust issues and flexibility goes right out the window.

As I just said, the Neck houses two very important aspects of the human nature—those of trust and flexibility. And, even though these two factors are both in the Physical body's jurisdiction, the Physical and Emotional members are very closely related, which means that the Emotional body is in direct communication with the Physical member at all times, leaving the Mental member, being devoted to past-future, out of synch. Even so, sometimes the Mental body likes to hang out in the penthouse of the Head area, thinking it is better or greater than its team members, merely because it appears to have a greater arena in which to play, having all of the past and all of the future at its beck and call—while not having any understanding as to just how huge the eternal moment of now actually is!

Unlike *faith*, which operates over a long period of time and is in the Mental's domain, *trust* is built moment by moment, like the mighty redwood tree. It can grow to great heights, but like that ancient tree, it can be cut down in a brief moment. And, given the conditions of life on planet Earth right now, with the various economic difficulties, natural disasters, and world governments in major change, we can all see how trust might not exactly be flourishing and how Necks might be rather tight.

Also, simultaneously, the Neck deals with issues of flexibility. Of course, if you are already non-trusting, it might be hard to have free-flowing flexibility as well. I will say that Mentally-based Beings tend to have a much harder time releasing hold of the Neck area, because trust is simply not in the Mental's awareness package. And, as I've said before, anything that is not in the Mental body's understanding (irregardless of whether the Being is Mentally- or Emotionally-based in its languaging) will always have a judgment, limitation, criticism, or negativity attached to it in tone, as the feelings are run through its system. It makes sense, really. *(wryly)* After all, if the Mental member can't grasp it—how could anyone?

Audience: *(sarcastic shouts of "Oh, yeah!" amid empathetic hails of "Hear! Hear! . . .")*

Astro: The Emotional body, on the other hand, can get direct input from the Physical as to simply knowing that it is okay to relax or not. But try telling that to the Mental nature.

Audience: *(hoots and hollers)*

(bedlam unfolds. . . .)

Foot: *(yelling)* Order please! Please settle down . . . . Quiet please. . . . There will be time for discussion later. Right now, please let our speaker continue.

Astro: *(purposely activating the participants)* Do we have any Necks who would like to say something? Over there to the left, sixteenth row back. Yes, you.

A Neck: *(with a sound of amazement in its voicing)* I've always wondered why I've felt so stiff and some days couldn't move at all. The thing is, I know it wasn't due to the way my Being slept, either. Now that you've shared, I realize that my Being is very scared, truly doesn't know who to trust, and doesn't even trust itself. Therefore, I live in a lot of pain constantly, and it's no fun at all. On the few occasions when the fear subsides, I feel a rush of energy and a lot more movement. Of course, I feel better now, after that process we did. Any chance you could tell my Being directly? He'll be here to pick me up at the end of the day.

Astro: *(amused at the idea)* Thank you for sharing with us, but no, as much as we'd like to help, your Being would only consider us to be interfering with him, and would likely go off immediately on the defensive. After all, *you* wanted to come to this symposium. Unfortunately, we still get very few Beings as yet desiring to come and listen.

(pausing to smile at the Necks who spoke) Anyone else? Okay, you over there in the middle section, in the back. Yes, please elevate your Self so we can all hear you.

Another Neck: *(full of gratitude)* I must be pretty lucky because I rarely get stuck. I think that my Being likes working outdoors, and that feeling runs through me. It's just not an effort balancing the Head, as her laughter keeps my cables loose. At night, I know I can release the Head and just let the thought energy flow through. And when my Being is upset, it doesn't last long, and so I don't get filled up with garbage. I'm sorry the other Neck is in such pain. I will definitely count my blessings now.

Astro: *(smiling broadly)* Thank you for your input. As we are all beginning to see, the Physical aches and pains that human Beings experience are not just from physical causes.

(the speaker pauses . . . as several Body Parts begin to look at each other from a new perspective. . . .)

Astro: *(in a strong voice, with a sense of nearing completion)* We've finally reached the Head area!

(a booming round of applause is heard)

First of all, in my work with people, as I place my hands on their Head with my eyes closed, I can feel the degree of activity going on inside. For people with the Mental base, quite often the vibration is very strong, almost like a hive of bees. Sometimes I can feel the protection energies as well. For the Emotionally-based Being, the Head can feel so full and hot that it is about to burst. From either experience, the Shoulders can stiffen and limit Neck movement—resulting in what I affectionately call membership in the Wear-Your-

Shoulders-for-Earrings Club. Progressing from there, when the Being and Its members are at full odds with each other, some folks enter the No-Neck Club. In these cases the Neck area shuts down and all creative thought originating in the Brain gets jammed, and Physical movement becomes blocked, locking the Neck in place.

A Head: *(jumping up and down on its seat)* Boy is that the truth! Sometimes I feel like the heavy pounding is going to split me open, and other times it feels so explosive that I think I'm going to pop.

Astro: *(also excited)* Aha! This is the tricky part—where the Mental and Emotional issues start to overlap. To you Heads here today, and even you Necks and Shoulders, I'd like to share with you one of the most common ways to produce this blockage.

First of all, for the purposes of creative imagery, let's say the Head is like a small theater, and all thoughts are like marbles constantly milling around inside. When someone yells "FIRE!" all thoughts jam into the exits or occipital areas, which are at the base of the Skull. Then those few thoughts who get through to the Neck—the equivalent of the freeway of life, usually four lanes each direction—they find that it has been closed down to one lane due to all of the re-construction needed when the Neck is in a locked position. Finally, thoughts reach the Shoulder area, which is like a disburse-ment center standing by ready to send the Mental member's thoughts out through the Wrists and Ankles, and to send the Emotional member's issues to be oozed out through the Pores of the Skin. The only problem is, by now these thoughts and concerns are upset, pissed off, unwilling to budge, and thus all backed up—until a Being looks like they are wearing their Shoulders for earrings.

(polite laughter)

So, let me ask some of you Heads here today, have you ever experienced your Being living only inside of you—and not consulting either of the Physical or Emotional partners?

A Head: *(nodding in agreement)* Oh, yeah—did you say that right! Why just last week, I was ready to push my Being out, because it was too crowded having *all* of its awareness just in my area. I mean, I appreciate the attention and all, but the pressure to be on or to have to find a solution to something gets really bad, and then she blames me for the pounding. How else can I tell my human to let go and give me the chance to create! I want to be noted, just like the next Body Part, but sometimes it's too much.

My Being is so serious, I'm not sure fun is even in her vocabulary. Quite frankly, it's news to me that I'm part of a team! I've been working alone for so long, I thought I was it . . . and quite honestly, it's been stressful and lonely.

Astro: *(moved by the sincerity of the Head's comments)* Thank you for sharing with us. When the Head pounds over and over, the build-up is coming through the Right Arm, spurred by Mental concerns. In the case of a full-blown migraine headache, the blockage is located in the Left Arm, containing Emotional issues. It is common knowledge that the Right Brain correlates with the left side of the body, and that the Left Brain relates to the right side of the Physical form. But even in the Brain, it might be said that it is the Mental and Emotional fluctuations that determine a Being's responses of pulsating pain, or full-blown pressure.

(Astro pauses to take a deep breath before summing up)

In conclusion, I'd like to say that once human Beings grasp and accept that people are *always* telling us where they are at—and I don't mean in just words, but even more so in actions; we will stop marrying potential, we will stop hoping our boss will change, and we will stop putting ourselves in situations that are disastrous for us. We will begin to operate from *what you see is what you get,* for it is only when *words* and *actions* match, and when all three members—Physical, Emotional, and Mental—are working together in harmony, that a Being operates in Its power.

On this subject of personal power, from what I've encountered in what I call my "mini-surveys"—that is, speaking only from my own observations—it seems that many of us aren't all that clear about our personal power. It's like this: only you signed up to be you, and you are solely in charge, no matter how often others think they have a greater say in your matter. However, other human Beings cannot support *you* until *you* support you—meaning you backing your full value, whether or not you fall short of your particular goal.

(wanting to make the point absolutely clear) Otherwise stated, when you show up in your full awareness of your personal worth or knowingness, others can claim their own, and are therefore less likely to attack you. Consequently, you are less likely to react to someone else's lessons or upsets, which gives them room to see their own life more clearly.

Realizing our power and acknowledging it is absolutely critical to our individual perception of a world that works for everyone, where everybody is accepted and appreciated for their contributions to the whole that we all are. This is especially true when we are prone to giving our power over to another to determine our worth. For example, this occurs when a person remarks, "I couldn't have done it without you." If you don't give their power right back to them by saying, "Yes, and you were perfectly capable of doing this all by yourself—I came along for the ride," and instead say, "You're absolutely right," then you have engaged in power-wielding over another. That is why power is so hard for humans to handle. Somewhere along the way those in power tend to begin to think they really *do* have a greater say in your life than you do, and they begin to believe themselves more powerful than others in life in general. When we begin to realize, acknowledge, and act from a basis of *personal* power, this factor alone will empower others.

In fact, coming "back" to the concept of BACKING OURSELVES, standing in our own power is critical to empowering others. Did you know that it is in our Mental body's jurisdiction to back each of us, the Being that lives in our body—our thoughts, feelings, and physicality—one hundred percent, *one hundred percent,* of the time. For example, picture the toy with the weight in the bottom that always returns to an upright position no matter which way it is pushed around: when we have the ability to stand in our own power, we know we are worthy, whether we do life right, wrong, upside down, inside out, topsy-turvy, or backwards. We, backing ourselves in our power, become a grounding ballast for others—and even though they bounce every which way around us, we hold center, and thus help them come into their own balance. It is truly a collegiate endeavor—one in which we can help each other, simply by being fully present and expressing that present Self.

To learn lessons, we are all asked to take risks, to go into the unknown, and experience the results. Failure has such a bad connotation, and yet it seems the lessons we learn through "falling short of the mark" seem to stay more firmly rooted in our consciousness. So, when we do get what I call "at-a-tilt," where one body is overactive, or one or two bodies are missing or underdeveloped, we can always realign through the two healing gifts each human Being possesses—laughter and forgiveness. By not taking the circumstances quite so seriously, and realizing that we, or possibly another, did whatever action we or they did without any malice of intent, we open the door to release that life experience and get on to another, more current one.

Again, you can realize by closing your eyes that you are a complete universe in yourself, which shows up in the world-at-large through your physical presentation, thoughts, and feelings. We are always "telling" people "who we are" by these three dense systems, which happen to be synonymous and beautifully synchronized with the universe-at-large, from one's own particular vantage point.

Just think of it: each of us is here to learn specific lessons, communicated in third-dimensional reality, through thoughts, feelings, and form—all interacting in a world agreed upon as a stage for each of our individual plays. From this notion, you might be able to "get" or internalize that we are incredibly orchestrated in such a fashion that all plays go on simultaneously just as though it were one Being wishing to experience Itself. Just possibly, any action on the planet is do-able by any one of us, either as a lesson learned, as one we are currently learning, or as one we have yet to learn. This is the basis for understanding and compassion, for if you have had a particular lesson, you are more apt to show compassion and understanding for someone undergoing that same situation. Conversely, if you have not yet experienced a particular lesson, you may have little tolerance for—or be downright short or impatient with—someone who is in the midst of that lesson. For example, if you are so fond of chocolate that you might call yourself a "chocoholic," when a day doesn't go by without eating some, you might better understand someone else who has a different daily activity that appears beyond their control.

To truly accept another requires both a similar experience *and* an understanding of the overall issue brought forth by that circumstance. Once such connection is made, acceptance follows. This outside acceptance is orchestrated by the integration of the three dense-body chairpersons. So, the integration or lack thereof of these our three dense-body chairpersons, makes all the difference in the world between working together on behalf of the Being and having a great day, or appearing in the world as competitive or an outsider, or looking to the world as though we are having a "bad-hair" day.

A classic example is the really brilliant children known as geniuses who were put ahead in school but who as adults are often considered socially inept, and who may have little or no personal happiness and contentment. So you see, it's not a case of one aspect of our nature (i.e., the Mental nature) being able to carry us through life, but rather three, fully participating members enabling us to integrate moment-to-moment living, which determines our expression of our Magnificence, as seen through each and every one of you Physical Body Parts, as well as the body as a whole. Plus, I've seen the level of integration affect abundant flow, safety, and full self-expression, as well.

So the larger the gap between word and action, and the wider the separation from totality, the more a Being must do to use Its energy or awareness to attempt to balance Its own at-a-tilt-ness as best It can (otherwise known as being "at effect" or reacting to circumstances rather than creating them).

That's why, historically, as long as people have not been allowed to fully "Self-express," we have developed beliefs such as "opposites attract"—as a means of filling niches that we perceive we lack within ourselves—in a desperate kind of hope of fulfilling each other by filling each other's holes. After all, why learn to change the oil in your car when you can marry a mechanic, or, more profound, why learn to express your emotionality when you can marry a very emotional person!

In truth, those perceived "holes" are simply lessons yet to be learned, and only to the degree we move away from the focus on opposites and begin to learn from a perception of whole-ness, do we begin to view all our lessons from a perspective of equal-ness, acceptance, and gratitude.

The further apart from Its center a Being gets, the stronger the counterforce must be. You see, human Beings are made of vibration and energy, and thus are not all bad or all good. Rather, the merging of the two creates the Light and Sound Beings that humans are remembering themselves to be, in the end fully represented in each of you Body Parts.

(. . . awestruck silence prevails as all Body Parts take in the magnitude of the incredible program called Life that they are

enrolled in, each part realizing that it—as Heart, Leg, Arm, or whoever—really does make a difference to the whole individual as well as its greater Self. . . .)

Astro: *(on a roll)* I'd like to share a notion related to Being-ness, as each of you holds a particular portion of a human Being. You might say I'd like to give you an expanded picture or sense of the totality in which each of you play an integral part. I have this idea that our male/female-ness is fourth removed from us as Being-ness or Source.

(a quizzical murmur breaks out in scattered parts of the audience at the words "fourth removed")

(quick to respond to the confusion) Bear with me, and I'll explain. When I speak of male/female issues being "fourth removed" from who we are, we can use the analogy of a tree. This particular tree has a large, sturdy trunk, with strong limbs and sturdy branches. At the end of these branches are some twigs. The Male/Female aware-ness is a twig to the tree of existence.

And right behind this twig is a branch called a human Being, and when someone's aware-ness moves off the small twig to this branch, they will not be able to view anyone as less of a human, and act accordingly—removing all abuse to women, children, and the Physically, Mentally, or Emotionally disabled—and the true meaning of *humane* will be evident.

And, lo and behold, when we move closer to the trunk of the tree by moving to a limb, where we are "Beings" who happen to be in human form, at this aware-ness we will ensure that all visual life is cared for—plants, animals, and the Earth itself.

Most startling to some, there is a place even under that aware-ness—the trunk of the tree—where everything "just is"—and from this aware-ness we see that even inanimate objects are cared for, as all visual aware-ness is equally "alive" as vibration and energy, and the only perceptible "difference" is that different "things" vibrate at different rates.

At that point of Universal Truth, all notions of past, present, and future, plus our idea of time and space, will not exist.

But don't worry, I don't see humanity realizing this last aware-ness anytime soon, so you as Body Parts needn't worry.

(several breaths can be heard being released throughout the room)

By the way, are we having any FUN yet?

(booming round of applause breaks out . . . and, oh yes, an uplifting ovation)

Foot: *(returning to the stage)* Thank you, thank you, Astro, for your most informative and inspiring lecture this morning. Just goes to show, when you begin to think you know something, you discover how little you do know. I hope you will stay with us for the rest of our annual meeting. You've definitely stirred up questions for me. And I'm sure that others here today feel as I do.

(the audience responds with another round of hearty applause)

We will now take an hour's break and give all of us a chance to stretch and interact. We'll begin again after lunch.

Wizard: *(squealing with delight)* Wasn't that something? That Astro sure gave us all a lot to chew on.

(Jaguar and Deer nod in agreement)

The Being: *(pondering aloud)* I sure wish we could get Astro aside and see if we can find out what we can *do* with the information we now have. I mean, all of what was presented is fascinating— but what do we do with it?

(Wizard, Jaguar, and Deer just gaze mutely at each other)

Your pain is the breaking of the shell
that encloses your understanding.

—Kahlil Gibran, *The Prophet*

When you have released the feelings that you have no way out,
you will have made an opening to find one.

—from *The Right Use of Will*

♡ CHAPTER FIVE ♡

SO, NOW WHAT?

*(. . . as the Auditorium empties, the Being catches a glimpse
of Astro and tries to work Its way over to the speaker. Even
while drawing near, the Being can't tell if Astro is a he or a
she. In fact, It concludes the Astral Body Therapist looks more
androgynous than anything else—slim build, long hair, but
no facial stubble. Actually, Astro has the face of a child . . . .)*

The Being: (rushing towards Astro) Excuse me, pardon me . . . excuse
me.

Astro: (a bit startled) Yes?

The Being: (bursting with appreciation) I wanted to thank you for all of
the wonderful information you shared with us this morning.

Astro: (in total control) Truly, I can do no more nor less than what I
am called upon to do.

115

The Being: *(not intending to be put off in Its errand)* Nonetheless, we were very glad, my members and I . . . *(looking around and discovering that Jaguar, Wizard, and Deer had momentarily disappeared)* . . . I mean, they were here just a moment ago. Anyway, we were glad to hear about the issues held by the various Body Parts and also wondering if you might have a moment to help us digest and integrate all that you alluded to in your talk this morning. You see, I've been trying to describe myself as a Being, and I quickly realized that I was quite at a loss as to how to do that in a way that others could understand what I meant by what I said—but frustration set in, . . . *(with rising agitation)* . . . and I didn't know what to do, and I got SCARED, and . . .

Astro: *(trying to defuse the Being's panic)* Whoa! . . . slow down. It can't be as bad as all that.

The Being: *(hollering)* Well, all that you said or implied was terrific— only, NOW WHAT? I mean, as we all know, everything is wonderful in theory. It's putting it into practice that's the hard part.

Astro: *(not affected by the Being's outburst)* Yes, that's quite true. Let me see if I have this straight. You say you were describing your Self as a Being, and you discovered you were not able to make a clear definition. Is that right?

The Being: *(still flustered)* Uh huh! And then, all of a sudden I heard this voice saying it was my Physical Body representative, there to help me, only I couldn't see it. So it asked me to listen to its duties and let my imagination create an image so I could see the member. And so I came up with a Jaguar—you know, one of those big jungle cats.

Astro: *(intrigued)* Oh my, do go on. . . .

The Being: *(without pausing to take a breath)* Well, Jaguar said that I really have three bodies that are in charge of my experience in third-dimensional living, and that the Physical body along with the Mental and Emotional bodies are just like a team and operate much like you mentioned this morning. And using the same process that we used for finding an image of a jaguar for itself, the Physical body representative described the attributes of the other two bodies, and eventually I saw a Wizard for the Mental body representative and a Deer for the Emotional body member. And, until just a moment ago, they were all right here beside me. I hope they are okay, as it is still so crowded here. . . .

(a look of pain crosses the Being's energy field as It looks around but cannot locate Its team players amidst all of the Body Parts leaving for lunch. . . . .)

(practically sobbing out loud) It's such a lost feeling not having them near.

Astro: *(looking closely at the Being and recognizing It as the one who brought order to the convention)* Why, if it hadn't been for you, my presentation wouldn't have been heard at this year's symposium.

(the Being's energy form brightens visibly for a brief moment, at this note of appreciation, but still quavers with uncertainty as the Being attempts to restore calm-ness within Its Self)

Astro: *(feeling both gratitude and sympathy for the Being)* The least I can do is help you and your body members . . . that is, of course, if we can find those members.

Jaguar, Deer, and Wizard: *(emerging from the crowd of exiting Body Parts and spying the Being with Astro)* Hey! Yo! Over here!

(a wave of great relief floods the Being's appearance)

What happened? We moved to get out of the way of some very hungry Body Parts and turned around to find you gone.

(before the Being can respond . . .)

wizard: I can't tell you how disconcerting it was!

Deer: I felt so abandoned!

Jaguar: Not to mention disoriented!

The Being: *(with glee, disregarding their distress)* Oh, it's so good to see you all again! As you can probably tell, I've been talking to Astro, who has most graciously agreed to elaborate on the information presented today—so we might better be able to integrate and operate as a whole. Astro, meet Deer, Wizard, and Jaguar.

(the Being's three dense-body representatives experience a momentary loss for words as their expressions of deep concern give way to the relief of having relocated the Being)

Jaguar and Deer: *(fully recovered and ready for the moment at hand)* Hi, Astro!

(Wizard, however, maintains a wary and slightly grim silence, still remembering the unsettled-ness caused by the separation and reminding Its Self of the necessity to be on guard against possible future mis-happenings)

Astro: *(with a sparkle in its eye)* Very pleased to meet you all. Shall we find a comfortable spot outside on the grass—perhaps under a tree—to chat?

The Being, Jaguar, and Deer: Sounds great!

        (they all file out of the auditorium and make their way across the street to a serene park area, where after settling into the grass, Astro begins to speak)

Astro: *(back in its professor mode)* First of all, I'd like to elaborate on the various vantage points and interests of each body member. I want to point out at the beginning that, upon first hearing parts of this information, you might not like some of the concepts I have to share. So, I ask that you keep an open awareness and suspend judgment until we've had a chance to share an entire experience together. For indeed, as you, Being, have already noted, information, by itself, is just interesting. It's not until this information connects to your personal experience that you can actually integrate your own support of you and your members through visible changes in the physical realm.

Now, let's move right ahead into the background of the three dense body systems. Since it seems that you, Jaguar, the Physical body representative, have been instrumental in getting us all together, as such, I'd like to share a little bit about your nature first.

(Astro pauses briefly to consider how to open the subject. . . .)

It's very difficult for you, the Physical body, to grasp why any portion of a Being's expression would *ever* be anything less than pure and supportive. You thrive on every body part being in good working order and able to enjoy participating in life. Am I right?

Jaguar: *(glad to be so understood)* Amen! I receive such great plea-

sure in being fully available to my Being—at least, until I get
fed up with Deer or Wizard here.

*(looks of surprise, confusion, and anger cross Deer's and
Wizard's faces . . .)*

Jaguar: *(silently noting that Deer and Wizard have withdrawn to
pout)* Anyway, as I was saying, I try to get along, and I even
encourage my team players to give up their narrow points of
view. But these vantage points seem to mean a lot to them,
which I simply don't grasp or understand.

Astro: *(watching the interplay of the three members)* I can see your
dilemma, Jaguar. Ultimately, you, as the densest body, have
the final say as to whether the Being has a form to play in or
not. And, in conjunction with that aware-ness, you also know
that the other two bodies can only reach the Being through
you. So, when either of your cohorts is upset or withdrawn, it
upsets your equilibrium.

Jaguar: *(shouting in agreement)* Boy, that's the truth! And when that
happens, I have to work so much harder just to appear as if I'm
all together!

(Jaguar glares at its partners)

Wizard: *(starting to speak and then thinking better of it, upon recalling several occasions when Jaguar had literally shut down—
because, as it had said, it didn't want to hear any more
explanations, recriminations, defensive comments, or judgments—particularly about Deer)*

(to itself) But how can you put total faith in a scared creature
like Deer?

(then, remembering Astro's request, Wizard decides to forego judgment just yet . . .)

Astro: *(anticipating their responses)* Now before either of you, Deer or Wizard, get all up in arms, I do want to let you know that any insights that I share about you are not made with any malice in mind. It just happens that after many millions of years in form, the human Being has developed very sophisticated ways to keep itself isolated and separate from the experience of wholeness. This was not intentional on its part, and it is not even on the conscious level, but the condition does exist and is quite prevalent today.

You see, not only are you three members designed to use your particular talents to integrate the Being's experience in form, but since the Mental and Emotional natures are one step removed from the densest body, the Physical, another quality has emerged over time as a result of the misperception of being separate. What has happened is that each person in form has developed a strength or point of view on life that is based either in the Emotional body's domain or in that of the Mental body. I refer to this as being either "Emotionally-based" or "Mentally-based." In other words, each point of view uses the same words in any language, but by those words they mean two entirely different things. It's like fruit. If the Mental nature is like apples and the Emotional nature is like oranges, both are delicious fruits, but they have yet to be blended into one fruit. To be more specific, the Mentally-based person might say, "You don't understand what I am *saying*," while the Emotionally-based nature could respond, "But you don't get what I *mean* by my words."

For example, do you remember the scene at the end of *Gone with the Wind,* when Scarlett finally "gets" that Ashley loved Melanie all along, and that she really did love Rhett? After running home, she lets him know. He says, "Why haven't you said so before this?"

And she replies, "Because I was hurt and wanted to hurt you back." This is a very Mental response to an Emotional issue. Then Scarlett goes on to say how she'll miss Melanie.

Rhett responds, "She was the only truly good person I knew."

To this, Scarlett remarks self-righteously, "Well, I loved her, too!"

Rhett says something to the effect of, "It was hard to tell by your actions," to which Scarlett retorts, "Of course I care! I always have!"

So, once again, the Emotionally-based Rhett and the Mentally-based Scarlett go around and around, talking apples and oranges, never gaining a blend of their natures, and, in the end, missing out on the love they shared.

The same is true for the two of you, Deer and Wizard.

(Deer and Wizard look up at each other, startled, by being singled out as though they each had just gotten caught with their hands in the cookie jar)

Astro: *(laughing)* I see that all this is still a bit vague. Let me give you some more examples to clarify what I'm talking about. For example, Deer, we could say that you operate laterally or horizontally, which means that if you, the Emotional body, are upset at home, you are likely to carry that upset all day— to work, to lunch, and home again. In fact, you might have noticed that any upset that is not cleared up immediately, stores within you *always as the present moment*—even if the upset happened twenty years ago. This is why something can happen today to trigger an old hurt or fear and leave you and the Physical body paralyzed—apparently for no logical reason.

Deer: *(in total disbelief)* How do you know that?

Astro: *(grinning like the cat that ate the canary)* Because it is true for all Emotionally-based beings—and also true for the Emotional nature in each of us, when not being overridden by the Mental nature. In the case of an Emotionally-based Being, if your upsets or concerns are not kept under control by the Mental body, you can find that you have gotten yourself into some precarious circumstances and then have to handle the consequences.

Wizard: *(interrupting in a huff)* Isn't that what I'm always telling you! You have to learn to think things through!

Astro: *(unruffled by Wizard's outburst)* Unfortunately, it is not in the Emotional body's jurisdiction to think about anything: it is *all* feeling and action. As you well know, the Physical and Emotional bodies are both *in the moment*, and they communicate directly at all times. In other words, Deer, if you feel so inclined, *you will give your all* in any one moment, without any thought to the future.

Jaguar: *(punching the Being's energy field)* Isn't that *exactly* what I told you?

(the Being hesitates and nods . . . remembering that those had been Jaguar's exact words)

Astro: *(leaning back onto the grass and clasping its delicate hands behind its head)* Now, to elaborate further about those human Beings who have an Emotional base . . . such Beings truly live in the moment of what they are doing. Their enthusiasm for a project or an upcoming event is real. However, in the next moment, they may head off in a completely new direction or forget the agreed upon meeting for that upcoming event—or simply want to do something else when the event arrives. If it is something that interests them, for example, a particular TV program that happens to grab them, they'll easily give it their full attention, as though they were in the program. The same is often true while reading a book. They are gifted with a strong momentary sense of confidence and sincerity and can easily get others to go along with their ideas—without any future knowledge of the practical application of such ideas. Unfortunately, the Emotional base can mean what it says in the moment (i.e., promises, enthusiastic agreement, etc.) with complete sincerity, but there is every possibility that it will feel differently by the time the event rolls around. Bearing this in mind, when dealing with an Emotionally-based Being, it is a good idea to check back with them, since their whole feeling about the venture may have changed 180 degrees. On the flip side, the Mentally-based Being prides itself on following through, keeping track of its commitments, and keeping its word.

The Emotionally-based have learned over the years that the Mental nature also prides itself on being right. So, these Beings tend to enlist the help of either a Mentally-based Being or an Emotionally-based Being who has a Mental override (as self-protection), asking the Mentally-based Being to provide several ideas on a project. And then, when the project doesn't turn out correctly, the Emotionally-based instigator might very well blame the person they asked to furnish them with the ideas in the first place!

Unfortunately, when a person is overwhelmed with their full Emotional impact, or depth of feeling, they can do hurtful things—without any perception of the consequences—just to get back at another Being, as though that will make themselves feel better. The Emotionally-based can be very good at roping others in, then feeling victimized or martyred, while blaming those others for any uncomfortable outcomes.

To the Emotionals' credit, however, if listened to, their intuition usually proves to be very strong and accurate, yet they tend to be quite sensitive and can get their own feelings hurt easily. Oh, and if they are around a very dominant Mental figure, they can live in a great deal of fear.

(at this, Deer looks up and sees Wizard glaring at it, causing Deer automatically to move backward in a slight retreat from the group)

Astro: *(seeing that a chord has clearly been struck between members, and deciding, in its customary bold way, to confront the issue head on)* You feel it, too, don't you, Deer? *(without waiting for an answer)* You see, what I am describing are the outer ramifications of what goes on inside the human Being, in your arena, am I not?

(Deer simply nods, unable to speak . . . .)

Astro: *(still playing the part of the instructor)* I have also noted that for many Emotional members, as well as for Emotionally-based human Beings, it can appear to you that the Mental nature has no heart or caring about your feelings—or even considers them unimportant next to its own creative thoughts. Does that resemble your experience, Deer?

(again, paralyzed in place . . . Deer nods its head in the affirmative, watching warily for some reaction from Wizard)

Astro: *(trying to bring Deer out of its cocoon)* Let me ask you this, Deer. Have you ever felt safe enough to tell Wizard exactly what was true for you, without reservation or fear of consequence?

Deer: *(a word faintly escapes from Deer's lips as it lowers its head)* No.

Astro: *(with great tenderness)* One last question, if you feel inclined to answer. What happens to you when you don't clear your feelings?

Deer: *(looking around at the Being, Jaguar, Astro, and Wizard and pausing a long while before speaking)* I get so frustrated and angry that I could scream—only who would listen? So I don't say anything, and I can feel the resentment growing. Before long, I don't want to do anything, and I don't have one nice thing to say to anyone! *(louder now)* And then I get so sad and feel so lonely that after a while, I say, why bother! And then I get lethargic and unresponsive. I slam the door shut between creative thought and physical manifestation and begin to operate like a robot. Every once in a while, I get the urge to come out and participate—but one snide comment or criticism, and I go under again. I mean, I feel like I'm drowning, and no one seems to notice. *That* is why it's so hard for me to get . . . *(with tears streaming down its face)* . . .when I'm all bubbly and up, people can't even see it's an act! Or, if they do see, they don't bother to stop and find out what's going on. So then I decide, if they don't care, I'm not going to care. So I actively set out to shut down my Heart—because it just hurts too much to be so isolated. Ultimately, I just pretend that nothing bothers me. . . .

(Deer pauses for a breath, not daring to look anywhere but at the lovely wildflowers growing in front of itself . . . then, finally, it lifts its head and sees four pairs of eyes also filled with tears. Not a one speaks, but when Astro reaches out to touch Deer, they all gather around, hug each other, and have a good cry.)

Wizard: *(venturing an apologetic word after all the tissues have been used and the tears have stopped flowing)* I had no idea of the richness of your feelings or the intensity of your caring! *(with a new tone of appreciation)* And I am glad to see that although you've tried, you have not fully shut me out. For if you had, you wouldn't have bothered to be so vulnerable now, would you?

Astro: *(impressed with Wizard's assessments)* They say—whoever "they" are—that love is a function of sharing what is true for you. However, they also sometimes neglect to say that it takes an actively *listening* ear to receive such a sharing and to complete the communication. How do you feel now, Deer?

Deer: *(without pausing and with more strength in its voice)* Much, much better, thank you. I feel lighter, as though a burden has been lifted. I mean, I know I was feeling heavy, but I forgot just *how much* I had stored away, . . . hoping that some day, someone would simply hear what I had to say as though I had value, too—and at the same time not *do* anything with my communication, just "get it" as my reality. Boy, am I exhausted! I didn't know just how much energy it takes to keep all of those feelings under the surface.

Astro: *(wandering in thought to another time and place)* This reminds me of a time when I was asked by a young Being to name the ten commandments. After careful thought and only being able to remember about six of the ten off the top of my head, I said, "For me, there is even a greater commandment than the ten we are familiar with, and that is: *Thou shalt not withhold thy Self.* This withheld love results in great Emotional pain, for love is all we are, no matter if we are living our truth in the moment or not. And, as you no doubt have memorized by now—it is up to each human Being's Emotional body to hold, as personal worth, that we as Beings are Incredible, Magnificent, Priceless Gifts of energy—whether we "do" life right, wrong, upside down or backwards, inside out or topsy-turvy! And we experience this knowing-ness of personal worth as LOVE, held physically in our Hearts, and backed one hundred percent by our own Mental members.

Deer: *(with tears of joy)* Thank you so very much, Astro, for considering my contribution to the Being of such value.

Astro: *(getting back to the matter at hand)* So now, Wizard, would you like to hear a little bit about the Mental nature?

Wizard: *(instantly on guard, retorting smartly with hackles raised)* I suppose so. But I do want to go on record that I try very hard to do my best at my job. You might have gotten the idea from Deer that I am cold and heartless, whereas I prefer to consider myself as practical.

Astro: *(suppressing a laugh at Wizard's seriousness)* It is so noted. And I know you believe it. . . . *(pausing briefly to focus its description)* Now, the Mental nature, unlike the Emotional and Physical, works *outside* of the moment. Therefore, it has the full wealth of the past, through memory, using hindsight to determine what is valuable. On the future side, it is designed to enhance possibility, through dreams and visions. After all, a Being must have dreams and visions to go forward in life.

Wizard: *(smugly satisfied with itself)* I'm glad you realize how important *my* input is to the Being.

Astro: *(continuing to paint the Mental's picture)* The Mental body keeps track of all of this data in a linear or vertical fashion, whereas the Emotional base experiences all things horizontally, across the board, all at once (as when a single item of upset ruins their entire day). The Mental nature can easily compartmentalize items, including upsetting notions, into neat, vertical stacks, where they can be stored for future handling without any bleed-over into the next event on the day's agenda. It's as if many Mentally-based human Beings carry around this huge ring of keys to see that all uncomfortable, embarrassing, or undesirable items remain locked safely out of view in their individual compartments. Or recall the example of the tip of the iceberg and how the Mental nature might say, "All is well," when the bulk of unresolved pain is simply submerged and out of view. The Mentally-based Being may even have the thought to get back to the stuffed-away item later, but that old cliche, "out of sight, out of mind," really does hold true, and so many items don't go away and therefore start to fill up what we call the subconscious, as habit energy. Even though we no longer think about the item or situation, we will still tend to operate habitually from it in our daily lives.

I must say that Mentally-based human Beings do tend to pride themselves on spending lots of hours, or even days, on figuring out the "right" way to do life. Some factors that go into these considerations are:

Number 1: Eliminate pain.

Number 2: Minimize embarrassment.

Number 3: Don't look stupid.

Number 4: Don't show hurt.

Number 5: Stay protected.

Number 6: Guard vulnerability, and

Number 7: Emphasize skills and talents.

To the Mental body member of the three dense systems, visual presentation is the most important facet in determining itself. After all, the Mental nature looks to others to see how it is doing, and it always wants to "look good" to others as well. It follows that the Mental nature is not fond of getting up in front of others to learn some Physical skill if it doesn't "know how" ahead of time, disliking to be "embarrassed."

In order to protect the Being, the Mental nature thinks it must run feelings through its doorway by judging, limiting, curtailing, or negating others. A typical Mental phrase (with Emotional upset being run through it) would be, "If you would just pick up after yourself, I wouldn't have to treat you like a child!" On the other hand, upsets that get stored in the various closets or compartments—which as you have already heard involves the Physical body—must be handled and cleaned out at some point. Bear in mind, however, in terms of the impact all this "stuffing away" has on the Emotional body—when it *appears* as though the Emotional body (or an Emotionally-based Being) has nothing to say, *look out!* A virtual time-bomb may be poised for an explosion.

At the same time, the Mentally-based being finds all of this emotionalism a bit out of control and undesirable. After all, once you are an adult, it's about time to put things in proper perspective, don't you think?—or so the Mental member advocates. As in the example given before of the Emotionally-based person who asks a Mentally-based Being for their input of ideas, the Mental member is usually more than happy to give its many ideas, but then gets stung and angry when that same Emotionally-based person comes back later and blames them, if and when those ideas didn't appear to work out. After several such occurrences, when it has just been trying to be of help, the Mentally-based nature may just decide not to share its ideas any more, especially if they are not going to be appreciated.

Wizard is right about the practical side of its nature. After all, if you've already spilled the milk, what *can* tears do about it? Nothing, really, but the Emotional nature is designed to relieve the pressure that builds up when an accident occurs or shock sets in. It can't do its job if the Mental nature curtails the process.

The Mental nature will tend, protectively, to try to "fix things," instead of allowing for the experience to enable the Being to learn a lesson and grow. Ironically, however, this just serves to hamstring itself, since only through growth can come greater understanding, compassion, and the experience of Love.

And don't forget the constant chatter that goes on inside the mind. As any active Mental nature will tell you, they have so much that they *don't* get around to sharing. Not surprisingly, the commonly held belief is that this chatter will always be a problem—so the popular notion is just to learn to live with it, ignore it, or override it with more desirable thoughts. After all, human Beings quite naturally are full of any number of points of view about anything or anyone, isn't that right? However, for many Mental natures, what often follows is that judgment becomes a way of life, something to "put up with," without recognizing that judgment results from one of our members trying to do the work of one of the others—and many times it is the Emotional body whose domain is interfered with.

(encouragingly) Does any of this apply to you, Wizard?

Wizard: *(with growing sincerity of interest)* I get your drift, Astro. Had I not just heard from Deer, I would probably be defensive, hearing you talk about me that way. But I am beginning to understand that when I go to protect Deer, which I consider to be a good thing, I also suppress its ability to do its own job. And, you are right also, in that I do seek right versus wrong and I am actively engaged in the process of getting others to agree with me. I can say I've even been active in a campaign to see that *I* am the most worthy facet that the Being uses to Self-express. In my zealousness to achieve, I would have to say that I haven't always paid attention to the Physical or the Emotional natures. After all, Jaguar always lets me know when I've gone too far, by shutting down with a cold or flu or such. But the Emotional system, I mean Deer, has usually appeared to me just to go along, too. How was I supposed to know I was being oppressive, when there was no verbal communication? And how was I to know how to deal with Deer's nature, when it doesn't tell me? *(Wizard finishes with flushed cheeks and arms waving)*

Deer: *(in a soft, barely audible whisper)* But I have tried to tell you, and you wouldn't listen unless I shouted or intimidated, like you, and that's not my *way* to Self-express.

Wizard: *(taking a LONG moment of thought and several deep breaths to keep from exploding all over Deer)... (with a tremendous effort at selfless-ness)...* I guess I'm realizing that I haven't really listened to you, Deer, for many years—not fully any-way, . . . and, an even deeper realization is that I now see that I haven't checked in with the Being, either.

(the Being, visibly moved, silently notes the insight)

Astro: *(feeling a shift in the Being and Its three densest team players)* Well, bear in mind that as human Beings we all have one thing for sure in common: we all mess up. Granted, some people do a better job of messing up than others, but that in no way takes away from our natural right to Self-express or from our "given" value, which is Priceless. When it comes to express-ing, as we've just heard, it just so happens that the Mental nature has different criteria than the Emotional member.

To sum up, at the risk of repeating myself, the Mentally-based person sees everything in a linear fashion: A, B, and therefore C. Or, in handling a problem or concern, this person would like to have all of the possible solutions brought out and placed on the table for consideration that can be thought of at the time in question. *Information* is the key to reaching these folks.

On the other hand, the Emotionally-based Being or member is another story entirely. Since the Emotional nature experiences things horizontally, as one continuous present moment, "across the board," an upset anywhere along the way could ruin or warp an entire day or more for them. The Emotional nature's main desire is to be "gotten" or "grasped" versus being understood. They are designed to flow and clear out debris, whether the stuck item is a blocked Mental notion or a jammed emotion. When they are full of feeling, this affects every aspect of their life, and they just want you to listen— with very few inputs—so they can release the frustration or anger or whatever. Truly, the Emotionally-based Being or member *just wants to be heard*, and all it takes is the listener's *full attention*, with only a few sounds or motions of acknowledgment—such as "Thank you," "What else?" or nodding the head—which indicate that they have been listened to and that the listener has received the Emotional body's communications. Then, the speaker can release all the anger, confusion, sadness, even joy or excitement, that has been building up inside the Physical form.

(taking a breath before continuing)

The Mentally-based response to the same scenario is more vertical: they can categorize or isolate portions of their life, such as work, home, recreation, school, and so on. Things can be fine at work, even while an upset is brewing in the home slot among their stack of compartments. For example, such a Being might be in the midst of an argument at home as the phone rings; they answer it as though everything is perfectly fine, without a trace of upset in their voice. Then, once they hang up the phone, the Mentally-based Being continues its language of blame, judgment, and criticism, until their emotions are no longer overflowing through the Mental body's domain.

In either scenario, once the Being's feelings have been expressed, all of the dense bodies can relax and reassess the situation. Both the Mentally-based person and the Emotionally-based Being have essential points of view, and a particular way of stating their vantage points. Neither is designed to override the other or to attempt to fly alone, but unfortunately they have come to that conclusion gradually over thousands of years of attempting to protect the Being from feeling isolated and appearing separate from other life and forms. So, not surprisingly, when asked to work together, all too often the two natures have no current experience or example that readily comes to mind that they can follow, and therefore they remain with no basis upon which to build such a change in belief systems.

For example, for you, Deer, like many Emotionally-based folks, how many times have you shared your point of view and just wanted to be heard, only to have the Mental nature (like any Mentally-based person) interrupt you by giving you all of the options you have: what to delete, what to add, as well as what to keep—according to them—and then gone on to say, "By the way, it's all so simple; just do A, B, C, and therefore D will happen." Maybe it's simple to them, but not to you, as you are about to bop them one!

(Deer glares at Wizard, recalling many such occasions when it didn't feel enough personal power to do anything about it)

Astro: *(quickly injecting equal support for the Mental body representative)* Or, from the Mental nature's (or Mentally-based Being's) point of view—like you, Wizard—have you ever shared all the gory details about the Being's break-up in a relationship, looking for some concrete way to resolve the situation, and all the Emotionally-based folks did was reiterate your upset? Big help they were!

Wizard: *(glad to voice an opinion)* It's so true! And after all the hours I put in to gather the facts and organize the details—quite accurately, I might add—can't these folks see that nothing can get done until you know what there is to be done!

(Wizard turns its full awareness on Deer to see that its message got received LOUD and CLEAR)

Astro: *(searching for a particular example)* For each of you, it's a case of feeling like, what's the phrase?—"My words have fallen on deaf ears." Or, "I'm just flapping my lips for my own benefit." Actually, when we're in survival mode—that is, disconnected, unconscious, and upset—we don't even hear ourselves!

Interestingly enough, as a general rule, ninety percent of what we say when we flap our lips is what *we ourselves* need to hear. Usually only about ten percent tends to be of value to others. *(chuckling to its Self)* I affectionately call human beings "lip flappers," for unlike other animals, humans are usually so busy flapping their own lips that they don't hear what they themselves or anyone else is saying!

So you see, depending on your base, the way in which your communications are given or received makes a huge difference as to whether you feel supported, or as to whether you think you've been helped.

Once again, I remind you of a very basic truth. The only person, Being, who is going to live their whole life with you, is you. Therefore, *you* are the person you want to please and to share and to be gotten or understood. In order to receive assistance from others, we have to *be behind* ourselves—that is, we have to *back ourselves entirely*. And we cannot give to others anything we have yet to give ourselves, whether it's support, love, attention, understanding, or the like.

Therefore, the more settled and present and integrated we are within ourselves, the more open and available we are to the world at large. (And all along, we thought they—whoever "they" are—just didn't like us!).

Bottom line, to have the world work for anyone, it has to work for all of us. Wherever we are, we all have to have our puzzle piece—our own particular contribution—be accepted and appreciated, not because it is better than another's, but rather because we are all complete wholes of the greater Self or whole—i.e., the puzzle—which we call the Universe that we live in here on planet Earth.

The Being: *(overwhelmed with the awe-ness of it all)* Wow. I had no idea how vast this notion of living is, or of my part in it. And I think I'm beginning to get a feel for my specific Mental and Emotional vantage points. But honestly, Astro, don't these differences make for some massive communication misperceptions between people?

Astro: *(showing its agreement by continuing the Being's line of speaking)* . . . not to mention the massive amount of energy it takes to sustain a Being whose members are at constant odds or miscues within itself!

Jaguar: *(in a sudden outburst, after having sat silently for so long)* Do you have any idea just how much energy it takes to hold two such bodies out-of-whack for so long???

(Astro pauses briefly, viewing Jaguar's wealth of feeling with new awareness)

Astro: Truly spoken, Jaguar.

(trying not to lose the cord of continuity)

In many ways, the Mental and Emotional natures have opposite orientations to the situations in life. For example, when the Mental nature sees someone doing what it wants to do, it asks, "How did you get there?" and looks to put "there" into a past-future context. In other words, it might recognize what steps are needed to approach that state, but it doesn't recognize what it is to BE there, or what "getting there" feels like. Likewise, although the Mental nature listens intently to the meanings of words that are spoken, it can never know whether the words "ring" true, because only the Emotional system recognizes whether something "rings true."

On the other hand, the Emotional nature "knows what it knows" in the moment—after all, it's just where it is, which is "there"—but it can't tell you to save your life what it did to get "there." In other words, it can't put into words or steps, what produced the result.

Thus, since identifying the steps in a process, following a set of directions, measuring or comparing anything and everything, or ordering priorities fall into the Mental's realm, it can readily tell whether a step or a piece is missing (along with identifying which particular ones), but then it doesn't have a clue as to how to go about *finding* the missing piece. Additionally, the Mental nature's strength is in possibilities and ideas, but, again, it cannot know whether those are connected and true, because that requires the Emotional member's strength of knowing what "rings true."

Conversely, the Emotional nature, rather than a specific awareness, has an intuitive "sense" that something is complete, true, or that a part is missing. This expresses as a vague uneasiness or the feeling of not quite being able to put a finger on what's missing, of not being able to describe it exactly. It may also "intuitively" be able to grasp or locate the missing item.

As another example, a Mentally-based person can have several things going on at once and be quite happy, while the Emotionally-based Being tends to prefer to give full attention to one thing at a time. On the other hand, the Emotional body member will give and give and give of itself—time, energy, finances, or skills—until, if it feels unsupported, it just stops. No forewarning, even to itself, and no signalling, generally speaking—such as "clue-ing in" the other person in a relationship as to just how bad they are feeling, or announcing that in exactly two weeks they will have *had it*—and no visit to the therapist, either. At this point, they are a done deal, and they will simply rearrange their life so as to exclude whoever or whatever was draining them of their life force (as they view it).

In terms of energy, the Mental body, being in charge of past memory and future dreams and visions, knows that it takes energy to fulfill these notions, and so it controls its energy flow, always trying to keep a little in reserve. If for some unconscious reason it is too fearful that it hasn't enough energy to create the desired results, it will automatically seek out or manipulate another person or situation to replenish its supply or take itself off the hook. For example, say a Being is a project coordinator and discovers that at four o'clock on Thursday there's more work to be done for the next morning's presentation than It has time to complete. In addition, two other people, embittered by not being chosen as coordinators, would rather see this Being fail than be willing to stay late at the office and help out. Meanwhile, the secretary, who's highly organized and efficient, has a date this evening. So, what's a Being to do? As the pressure mounts from within, and at a loss as to how to ask for support from others who have different perspections on the problem, the Being thinks its only alternative is to coerce someone into lending a hand, through scheming and plotting, instead of a direct, honest appeal for help.

The Emotional nature, on the other hand, functioning solely in the moment, may choose at any time to give its all with no regard for future needs. An example of this would be evident in dating. Two people, new to each other, wanting to impress the other and enjoying each other's company, one thing leads to another, and before either has really thought about it, they find their feelings overriding the fact that neither of them have any kind of birth control or other protection, and they become intimate anyway. In this scenario, the Emotional body can consider any Mental input as cumbersome and possibly inter-fering with their full attention, love, empathy, compassion, and support—not to mention enjoyment—that rules the mo-ment and later may seem to ruin the future if an unwanted pregnancy occurs.

In both cases, when one body overrides or ignores the input of the other, we, the Being, living in a Physical form, are literally left at-a-tilt with the world around us.

This at-a-tilt-ness can result in some classic points of view. An overriding Mental body remark might be, "Why don't those people who *think* they know it all, stop upsetting those of us who do!"

It's easy for Mentally-based people to see discrepancies in others, but rarely do they discern the same inconsistencies in themselves. They are typically other-directed, critical (running their feelings through the Mental body), and they habitually point out others' faults to keep the focus away from themselves. It hasn't occurred to them that the person in front of them is a mirror for themselves. In addition, the Mental nature will turn right around 180 degrees and do the *exact* thing they've been criticizing in another, which just adds salt to the wounds of the one on the receiving end of the criticism.

This unconscious habit—of disliking and judging in another the very thing, action, or characteristic that they turn right around and do themselves, without seeing the connection—results in the Mental nature's words and actions *not* matching, and then all hope of gaining *trust* between the parties involved goes right out the window.

Deer:	*(boosting its amps)* That's EXACTLY what you do, Wizard, all the time!
Wizard:	*(incensed)* Don't be ridiculous! If left up to you, we would be embarrassed ALL of the time.
Deer:	*(really gearing up now)* See, there you go AGAIN, putting the blame on me. How do you expect me EVER to want to work with you, when everything you have to say about me is so derogatory?
Wizard:	*(in total defense of its actions)* Who says I DO want to work with YOU? Quite frankly, I don't see anything in you to

which to offer up my admiration and respect. You are such a WIMP!

Deer: *(absolutely white with rage)* That's not true! Take it back—or I'll NEVER speak to you again!

Astro: *(turning to the Being, merely as a point of reference)* Say, doesn't this conversation remind you a little of good ol' Harry and Frank?

The Being: *(chuckling to Its Self)* If I didn't know better, I'd be upset for them not noticing that their sole job is supposed to be to serve me.

Astro: *(catching the humor)* Well, that's okay, because, in truth, as we might want to note here, it is only IN THE MOMENT OF THE UPSET that the Emotional body actually grows!

(Astro, the Being, and Jaguar wait patiently for Deer and Wizard to retract their claws. As the dust settles, Astro, clearing its throat gently, shifts the focus of attention by continuing . . .)

Another classic response of the strongly Mental nature (in this case one who has no conscious awareness of Emotional contributions), when it wants agreement, might be to say to an Emotionally-based person (who differs about something the Mental said), "Quit lecturing me!"

Or, "Why are those foreigners over there being so rude by talking among themselves in their own language? Can't they at least speak English in public—after all, this is America!" Of course, the Mental nature, being the center of its own universe, thinks that the foreigners had to be speaking about It, otherwise they would have spoken in English!

Or, another typical Mental notion would be, "If they really loved me, they wouldn't sell the ranch . . ." or "leave me with the grandparents . . . ," or whatever. Such statements results from the Mentally-based person's tendency to determine love through actions, while the Emotionally-based person assesses love through the quality of the interaction, based on the touch and tone of words and on the degree of "presence" with another.

To the Mentally-based Being, the best defense is a good offense. A good example is the person who has learned to survive by adopting the behavior and attitude, "I don't have ulcers, I give them." You might recognize this offensive defense tactic as an accepted and valid form of reasoning in our law and court system—as if the truth can be found without considering Emotional input or impact. The idea can be understood in theory, but in this case, life and theory simply don't match, for we are not separate from our feelings, any more than we are from our thoughts or our actions.

In the same vein, not surprisingly, how we view others determines how we sound. Our Mental nature focuses on the meanings of the words we use, but our Emotional nature picks up the tone and the touch of the words. If we don't like someone, it is evident in the tone and touch of our voice. So, when someone must be strong and very responsible, and they don't want to be, their words sound short and clipped, and the tone is harsh, as when a retail sales person says, curtly, "Do you need any help!!!" Without understanding why, we tend to respond with a quick, "No, thank you!" because the touch and the tone of the words was not fully supportive, even sounding unfriendly.

The Being: *(interrupting with an entirely different thought)* Excuse me, Astro, but you briefly eluded to an Emotionally-based Being with a Mental override. What did you mean by that?

Astro: *(smiling happily at the Being's level of listening)* I'm so glad you asked. This instance fits in with the notion of the 'absent-minded professor,' doesn't it? *(laughing at its Self)* Or perhaps it's just another strain of Sometimer's dis-ease. I do seem to have a habit of sharing bits and pieces of ideas and then forgetting that others might not know what I mean by them.

To answer your question, Being, the Emotionally-based nature with a strong Mental override or control is someone who was bombarded Emotionally early in life and simply couldn't maintain their natural base. What I mean by bombardment is hearing phrase after phrase that undermines one's sense of worth—for example, "Pick up your feet!" and similar remarks repeated with a tone that insinuates that you're too stupid to figure it out for yourself. Other examples might be, "You're so clumsy!" "Quit fidgeting—just sit there and shut up!" or "You're so stupid; you're never going to amount to anything." When, as a sensitive child, the Being hears these comments over and over again, there occurs a moment when doubt enters the child's consciousness, and in that brief moment, they believe these statements to be true. So, for survival reasons, they must protect the Being they are, and they turn themselves over to the protection of the Emotional's counterpart, the Mental nature. This is like having always to speak a second language instead of your native tongue.

By the way, this particular scenario is the most difficult to recognize in people, because you might think you are talking to a Mentally-based Being, yet you can't understand why they don't respond to reason and also hide their feelings! In life, these folks tend to undercut or curtail themselves by constantly pulling the rug out from underneath themselves before someone else can do so. The result is a lot of denial on all fronts. For example, you might say to someone, "Wow, don't you look great in that dress!" And the person responds, "Oh, hardly, not in this old rag." Another example would be, "I've never seen someone so talented with fixing cars," and the person brushes away the compliment with, "Oh, I'm just tinkering." Each time a compliment is sent, the person designed to receive it deflects it away from themselves. After all, as their thinking goes, if you really knew them, you'd know they were not particularly worthy or capable. Their tragic double bind is that since they unconsciously find themselves unable to fully receive acknowledgment and gratitude, they in turn cannot fully give or express appreciation to others, either.

It is quite common to find abandonment issues strongly present in many Mentally-based Beings, as well as in the Emotionally-based who have strong Mental overrides—as the Mental nature, while providing the Being with protection from experiencing such deep feelings, also imprisons the "Self," impairing the very means by which we are able to feel connected and loved.

In extreme cases, when the Mental nature rules with the Emotional input deleted completely, this creates our serial killers or premeditated revenge. Once the Mind convinces the Being and overrides the other two systems completely, there is nothing to stop it from achieving its goal except outside stimuli. After all, the Mental nature, being outside the present moment, doesn't experience consequences, even those of its own creation.

On the other hand, when the Emotional nature seizes complete control of the day, it can result in religious fanatics or very successful con artists—for indeed they do believe in their cause or venture above all other options and considerations, getting you to believe in it, too.

Either way, a detrimental physical occurrence happens. If the Mental body is on the rampage, the Emotional outcry of others in the society will eventually get the energy stopped. If the Emotionally-overridden nature gathers an extreme amount of momentum on its wave, the legal system will eventually step in to save the day, often amidst the disapproval of those who have been utterly swept up in the wave.

Bottom line, all of us are influenced by our family or lack of family situation, by the environment, and by circumstances, but not a one of us was born to be off-balanced. Being at-a-tilt is something we all have learned and which all we deal with differently.

The Being: *(growing despondent)* With things so out-of-whack, is there any hope of getting into balance? Is it even possible to get to a place of cooperation? I mean, if it has taken a human Being like myself eons to get to this place of disruption within the Self, what can be done to remove these habitual patterns? And as you just said, apparently most of them aren't even on the conscious level.

(in exasperation) What's there to make a person ever want to clear these avenues of expression, let alone admit to them in the first place?

Astro: *(chuckling)* MY, my, my . . . such serious concerns for one Being to hold. The good news is that everyone's members are always *around*, even if they haven't been used in years—and even if they have been discounted a lot. Also, not only do we as Beings naturally wish to be appreciated for having the courage to show up in form and be treated naturally with admiration and respect, but so do our three foundation members through whom we Self-express. And always remember that no matter how much it has been curtailed or abused, **the Being itself cannot be harmed.**

That being a given, first and foremost it is necessary to clear the built up resentments, angers, and fears, before starting the realignment process between the members. After all, if you have termites in the wood flooring, remodeling the rest of the house is almost pointless.

Also, it helps to realize the fact that much of what people store up as hurts and resentments may be largely due to language misnomers or misperceptions, which takes place through our rearranging the truth to fit our particular belief systems. Fact is, how we see things or remember them may not be *the* Truth, nor may it be how the other team member or person viewed the same incident. As I often say, as a means of minimizing getting stuck in such misnomers or misperceptions—and this is certainly true about all I've shared today: "I speak for me, because I am the only one who can; the same is true for you."

I've often said that I fully support anyone having any point of view they choose, but I draw the line when they think I must take on their point of view, especially of me. What I hear and choose to focus on instead is that they care, so I address the caring by saying, "Thank you for caring enough to tell me that," "Thank you for bringing that to my attention," "Thank you for repeating yourself," or "Thank you for sharing." Indeed, even the worst teasing, whatever that is to you, is simply an effort to share. However, we have gradually been losing our sense of gratitude, and therefore our ability even to *want* to interact can go by the wayside at times.

So what do you do when someone comes steam rolling over you with their point of view? As I say to my clients, when a Mack truck comes your way, and you are out in the street in its line of destruction, don't freeze and get run over by stopping to defend or explain yourself. Simply step aside, and let the judgments or tone of voice or other denials just go on by. Acknowledge the fact that they cared enough to share their point of view, but don't think you have to give them an explanation, take on their ideas of you, or get hooked into thinking you have to be less than yourself to function on the planet!

Furthermore, it's handy to bear in mind, when listening to others, that Emotionally-based and Mentally-based issues will arise in the person's voice and language. The Emotionally-based Being will speak for itself, whereas the Mental or Mental-override will place the conversation outside itself and talk in generalities, tending to disparage or outright attack "others." To point up the interaction in a humorous way, if you find yourself the object of such an attack, just remember that when someone throws trash in your temple (i.e., towards your Physical form), you can always remind them that the garbage can is down the hall.

(the Being and its members chortle amongst themselves, recalling instances when the line might have been well-employed)

It helps to remember, as you listen to others speak, that the Mind works overtime to think things through and "do life right"—sometimes Dead Right, if carried to an extreme degree of isolation from the rest of the Self. However, like all of us, *it simply wants to be acknowledged for its efforts.* Whether we take its ideas on or not is *not* the crucial point.

Another means of helping your own members realign, as shared earlier, is to regularly employ various means of moving stuck energy, such as vocalizing, working up a sweat through hard physical exercise or work, and various other means, as we covered during this morning's general session of Body Parts. When you are dealing with your own members—or even the Physical, Mental, or Emotional natures of others, now that you know something about how they generally express their particular points of view—it also helps to know that you can speak to those natures *directly*, just as you can talk to Deer, Jaguar, and Wizard here, knowing that they are the representatives of your three base systems. For example, you can say, "Thank you for sharing, Mental nature," if you notice that you have been criticizing yourself or another in your mind.

Along the same lines, it is extremely important as you go along from day to day to "complete" with people—that is, if things don't quite resonate for you, to ask questions to gain clarity as to a person's intent or meaning. "Completing" also means saying all that you have been meaning to say and doing all that you have been meaning to do in reference to that person. For example, have your physical actions matched your words to that person? Otherwise, those incompleted items get stored along with all other unprocessed, unclarified, or unresolved thoughts and feelings. Being "complete" with every relationship doesn't mean the relationship is done or over; it just has to be brought up to date, with nothing stored. Likewise, just as completion doesn't mean "done," clarity doesn't have to mean "agreement." This frees you up to be more present in the Eternal Moment of Now, and not have to carry all sorts of unresolved people, statements, and items around with you.

The good news is, by whatever means it occurs, once reintegration amongst the members takes place, a Being uses a lot less energy being *on* track than it does in being off. So, when words and propelled actions match, we all become Living Examples of a whole Being, and we can get on with the wonder of being in form.

At this point, a Being experiences itself, not only as full and complete, but also overflowing with joy, enthusiasm, support, love, etc., to share with others—and not surprisingly, once a Being maintains its sense of being an Incredible, Magnificent, Priceless Gift, it will no longer allow for doubt to enter as to its value—and judgment, criticism, negativity, and limitation will no longer rule the day.

The Being: *(somewhat reassured but still feeling anguish and overwhelm)* Well, I certainly would like to get to such a point, but, with my members out of sorts, how can we even get started on such a venture?

Astro: *(in a reassuring tone)* Not to worry, Being. Even though the "hands-on" route through the Physical is the most "get-able," we can reach you, the Being, through any of the bodies—Physical, Emotional, or Mental.

The Being: *(with interest piqued)* "Get-able?"

Astro: *(sharing frankly)* Yes, in my work, the Physical route provides the most direct means through which both the Being (on the massage table) and myself can work together, because *safety* is in the Physical body's jurisdiction. Once the Physical system considers the intrusion of my vibrational energy as one hundred percent safe, it will most often by-pass the Mental and Emotional holding or control patterns.

              Remember, the Physical body does not pass judgment. It is literally unaware of any need to protect itself until the moment of impact. Only then, in the moment, as it registers the fall, ache, pain, or injury, does it realize there is something to deal with, whereas the Emotional and Mental body members, being less dense and living inside the Physical form, recognize that some of life's experiences are preferable over others. The Emotional body remembers this only when another item or situation has triggered a withheld hurt. For, as you are learning, all Emotional items not expressed from the past are still held *presently* in the Physical form.

              As I mentioned before, an Emotionally-based Being, even though the Emotional body is always in the moment, can protect its "Self" by withholding its communicative feelings, thereby reducing vulnerability.

              However, right now, Being, as long as you know or sense that the Physical body representative definitely feels safe at this moment—is that correct, Jaguar?—

Jaguar: *(noting its own tingling sensations)* Oh, yes indeed!

Astro: *(smiling broadly and giving Jaguar a nod of acknowledgment)*—then, through a couple of experiential processes, which I would love to share with you, we can look to bring all of your members not only up to speed, but ready to work together with you! Would you like that?

The Being: *(beaming)* Oh yes!

Astro: *(quite intensely focused on the Being)* However, to proceed, I must ask you, the Being, to let go of your current pictures of your Self and your members, and to continue without their input.

(Wizard, Deer and Jaguar look sadly at the Being, since, aligned or not, they are all quite fond of each other. The Being, not knowing if Its members would ever appear in this way again, gives each of them a long hug and thanks them profusely for helping It to become more conscious of Its Self.)

If the doors of perception were cleansed,
everything would appear as it is—infinite.

—William Blake

I may not be able to change the world I see around me,
but I can change the way I see the world, within me.

—Brock Tully, *Reflections for Someone Special*

If you dwell on the past, you rob yourself of your present,
yet the seeds of our destiny are nutured by the roots of our past.

—Master Po, "Kung Fu"

♡ CHAPTER SIX ♡

THE INTERNAL VIDEO LIBRARY

Astro: *(whose form is relaxing against the trunk of a large, shady tree, addressing the Being)*

I affectionately call these ventures a journey into your internal Video Library, followed by a visit to your Official Board Room. After all, each of us perceives the very same information from a different vantage point and from different responses to a variety of circumstances. I will remind you, here and now, that I can't make you view the information that surfaces in any particular way, nor would I choose to do so. I may suggest possibilities, but only to stimulate your own natural creative juices. Again, I ask you to release any preconceived notions and to allow your natural creative juices to flow. If at any time during this process you lose your connection with me, please wave your vibrating hint of a hand above your energy field and I will be sure to stop and give you time to re-align. After all, how the information that comes forward appears to you, may affect you in ways you haven't imagined until now. In any case, you know from experience that the way to express your point of view is through your three dense bodies and the integration of their functions.

Remember, there are no right or wrong awarenesses, only observations. So sit back, relax, take a few deep breaths, and let your voice out with a long, drawn-out sigh. . . . A-a-a-a-a-h-h-h-h, yes . . . and know that the following journey is an opportunity to shift your perceptions in a way that allows for a renewed view of reality, an expanded vision of life possibilities—and a personal transformation.

(continuing after a brief pause)

I'd like to have you take your imagination to a beautiful plaza nestled among some really tall buildings. As you look around, I want you to notice that, unlike most cities, there are no homeless, and no noisy traffic or hustle and bustle. This just happens to be a park-like area surrounded with several office-type buildings. It is a lovely plaza, multi-leveled with fountains, reflecting ponds, sculptured bushes, and pruned rose bushes of many varied colors—all surrounded by two-brick-high planters, leaving plenty of room for walking. On an upper level, there is a huge fountain, also encased in brick, with sun-reflected, rainbow-and-bright, multicolored water splashing leisurely within its circumference, which provides a soothing, refreshing sound.

(pause)

I'd like you now to look around and notice that among these really tall buildings there is one building so tall that it goes way up into the clouds. This is your very own office building, the one we are going to visit today. So I want to ask you how you would like You, as Essence or Being, to be dressed today. This is so that, should we come into contact with any of your employees, we will be seen and recognized as the owner of this building's business. You might want to wrap yourself in sparkling light. Or perhaps you would want to dress casually with no shoes on. Another possibility would be to up your vibrations just enough so that your hint of form is more visible. Or, then again, you might prefer to dress up in an Evan Picone or Giorgio Armani or Chanel suit with matching accessories. As this is your endeavor, how do you wish to be seen today?

The Being: *(looking skyward as it ponders the question)* Well, I'm a rather casual Being, so I'd like black leggings with a baggy T-shirt that has a picture of multi-colored starbursts on it, and bare feet.

Astro: *(continuing with its eyes closed, to keep the internal vision present)* Okay, now that you have dressed your Self, I'd like to have you walk up the cement steps to the glass doors leading into your building and then enter the lobby. You will immediately see one lone elevator to the right, which will later take us to the top floor, where your board room is.

For now, however, on the left, you can see several elevators that go to all of the floors short of the top floor. I'd like you to take one of these elevators up to the third floor.

(pause)

As the doors open and you step out, please head toward your right, down a long corridor that has doors leading into rooms on both the left- and right-hand sides of the hall. The door we are looking for is the one marked The Video Library. Once you have found it, just note whether yours was found on the left- or right-hand side of the long hallway, and enter the room.

As with most libraries, you see long rows of metal shelving. Here in this room, these shelves hold the master copies of your life's videos. These video masters are stored in huge metal canisters with labels, just like motion picture reels in a movie theater. Each section deals with a different aspect of your life as you recall it. Now, before we proceed, I'd like to mention that behind the door to your video room and off to your left is a huge shredding machine that empties into a big metal bin. This bin is situated so that, once we have shredded a particular item, it will go into this huge metal incinerator and be burned.

So now, I'd like for you to go down the aisles of some of your issues. For example, you might find a whole section called Self-Esteem. As you browse through the large cans of video tape, you might find one marked *YOU'RE TOO LOUD!* or *YOU'RE TOO INQUISITIVE*, or even *YOU'RE ALWAYS IN THE WAY*—whatever it is that you recall hearing growing up which affected your support of yourself.

(pause)

The Being: *(thinking out loud)* Let me see . . . oh, here's one: *KEEP QUIET AND QUIT BOTHERING ME!* and in subtitles, *MY POINT OF VIEW DOESN'T MATTER.*

Astro: *(enthusiastically viewing all from within)* Great, so now pull it off the shelf, expose this master tape to the brightness of the room, unroll the film, put it into the large shredding machine, and watch it come out in tiny little pieces into the metal bin. Now, you have the option to burn the shredded tape right away or wait until there is more in the bin and burn it all at once. If you know anything at all about film and negatives, you will know that it burns quickly. Do yourself a favor and unroll all of the video tapes you can see that relate to poor Self-worth.

The Being: *(right in the midst of judgmental accusations)* You mean like *YOU'LL NEVER AMOUNT TO ANYTHING*—or *ANY NIT-WIT COULD FIGURE THAT OUT!?*

Astro: *(realizing that the Being's feelings have been tapped, and with great compassion)* Yes, they are all related to your sense of value. After all, we are all a bit habitual or robotic by nature, and after we have heard something in words or had it implied often enough, we are going to believe it somewhere along the line. Keep looking in this section for all of the items that you can spot by label on the video cans, pulling those tapes off the shelf, exposing the films, and shredding them.

The Being: *(really getting into Its Emotional and Mental pain)* How about *YOU NEVER THINK OF OTHERS*? And here's a good one: *WHY CAN'T YOU BE AS COORDINATED OR AS INTELLIGENT AS YOUR BROTHER?*

Astro: *(validating the Being's experience)* Yes, all of these phrases or implied statements negate your Magnificence, and after a while you will forget that *any* Being in form, including you, is an Incredible, Magnificent, Priceless Gift . . . just by being here on the planet! And, furthermore, even though your Being may have received curtailment, non-support, blame, or antagonism—your worth remains intact no matter what.

The Being: *(in clearer awareness)* Now I get it. All of these attitudes or energy fields have been bombarding me for so long that some have gotten inside me, and now I falsely believe these notions to be true for me—as well as for others.

Astro: *(in full support of the process)* Exactly. So, when you are ready, I'd like you to move on to another section, perhaps to an aisle labeled Physical Appearance. For example, here you might find some time-worn titles such as *YOU'LL ALWAYS BE FAT* or *YOU'RE UGLY!*—or how about *YOU'RE CLUMSY*. Some other possibilities might be *YOU'RE A GOODY TWO-SHOES*, or *YOU'RE NICK-NAMED 'FOUR-EYES'*, or *YOUR CLOTHES ARE TOO SMALL (or LARGE)*, or maybe, *YOU'VE GOT TWO LEFT FEET!*

Please remember, you don't have to make anything up. Just look at your library shelves and see what comes into your mind's eye. *(pause)* Then open the can, unroll the film, shred it, and burn all the scraps when the bin gets full.

(With that complete support from Astro, the Being searches down each aisle and removes quite a number of videos, such as YOU'RE TOO SENSITIVE *and* YOU AREN'T MOTI-VATED ENOUGH! *plus* YOU'RE TOO THIN *and* YOU'RE GOING TO BE AN OLD MAID, *and* YOU'RE

TOO AGGRESSIVE!, *taking great pleasure in releasing these hidden holds on Its natural, abundant flow.*)

Astro: *(continuing to create a safe space for the Being to completely take off Its holds on buried thoughts and hurts)*

This process is a little bit like popping popcorn. It is a little slow at first, as the gates to all of the stored-up feelings associated with these thoughts begin to open, until finally *all* of the curtailments and limitations that have been placed on our Magnificence and that have challenged our individual ability to dodge these bullets, can be lifted. When we have finally completed searching, finding, and destroying these tapes, this leaves us free to look freshly at our lives and *choose the qualities we want* to experience and share with others. And then, eventually, the awarenesses (again, these are held by our own perception, no one else's) will slow down again as you realign with your Self.

(the Being continues to check each aisle, emptying canister after canister . . .)

Astro: *(adding in the understanding to back the newly-unfolding perceptions)* In this particular process, I am only giving you suggestions as to what might be on your library shelves. Remember, each of us have different receptors to any situation and, since we each have different lessons to learn, we focus on different points of concern or revelation. The beauty of it all is that, like a jigsaw puzzle, all of the parts are wanted and needed for the puzzle to be complete. Therefore, it will take *all* of the human Beings on this planet to grasp their worth, to see that this planetary experience is complete. So, it is not sufficient simply to clear your own internal closet, but rather, once cleaned out, what is called for is to go on to be a Living Example for others, by encouraging them to do the same. This will tend to free up others' energy to more fully make their own unique contribution to the whole, allowing everyone to feel supported in that process and to feel good about themselves.

(pause)

Be sure to go down as many aisles as you can see, and even those way in the back that are harder to get to. If need be, let yourself take a flashlight to those video tapes that are all dusty and hard to read, way in the back corners. Some of these might be categorized under Family, Motherhood, Self-Worth, Provider, Intelligence, and so on. Only you know those phrases that you heard during your growing up years, and from which direction or person you heard them. I want to make one thing perfectly clear: we are not here to place blame on another Being, who is also a Magnificent, Incredible, Priceless Gift, whether they present themselves in that light or not—but we *are* here to clear out how you hold others and issues, inside your Physical form. It's just like the amphitheater process that you led us through earlier, Being. The suppressed hurts and feelings that often accompany our interactions with someone we love do not damage our love for that person. However, the removal of these hurts and feelings does free up how we view them. To one person, a phrase could have little impact; to another, that same phrase and how it was said could have debilitating results.

(the Being hesitates, not feeling sure about venturing all the way to the back shelves . . . . after all, those items are sure to

be securely hidden in the subconscious, and the Being isn't at all sure about wanting to disturb them)

Astro: *(opening its eyes, aware of the Being's discomfort)* Another wonderful aspect of this process is that you don't have to tell anyone what is in your Video Library. In fact, before we are through, we will be dissolving the entire room. So don't worry if you think or feel you haven't gotten it all. Just be sure to expose the film from any video canister that you do happen to find, with whatever label it says—just unroll it, shred it, and then burn it.

(pause)

You will be surprised at how much weight this lifts from your internal closet, which by the way sometimes results in a lightening of your physical form as well.

(another pause, as the Being continues to locate and destroy cans of videotape)

Astro: *(encouragingly)* So, Being, how are you doing in clearing out your old videos?

The Being: *(astonished with the whole process)* My, oh my! My room was huge. It took me a little while to start imagining the picture you were painting for me, but then I jumped right in. Before you even got to the different sections of issues, I could see *DON'T TALK SO FAST, DON'T TALK SO LOUD,* and *SLOW DOWN.* I could feel anger surfacing as I pulled those videos off the shelf, unrolled the film, shredded them, and— without waiting for other items—burned them all.

I mean to tell you, I have almost felt persecuted by family, teachers, and friends, who I thought, by their repeating of these phrases with a disapproving tone, wanted me to match *their* ideas of me, instead of accepting me as I am!

And right after that I saw *I DON'T HAVE WHAT IT TAKES TO BE A LEADER* and *I NEVER HAVE ANYTHING WORTHWHILE TO SAY.* Amazingly enough, for as many tapes that I found which were produced and directed by others, I also unearthed stacks and stacks of films that had been written, produced, and directed entirely by myself, no one else. So obviously, I was also having some trouble crediting, or even knowing, myself as I am! And I could see that with all of these tapes running over and over again, I never felt that I amounted to much—and for sure, I wasn't okay as me. It's as if there's this hidden code that everyone has to follow in life called "Normal." And I've always been referred to as weird, crazy, or too selfish. And all the while, I knew that, to me, Normal meant Boring. And I just couldn't stay interested in doing life the same way, day in and day out. In fact, I have to laugh at myself at the many times I have made lists and routines, and then proceeded not to follow them. I like adventure—nothing too outrageous mind you— but a little flair to life. I was almost convinced that this attitude of mine was wrong, and so I've tried to fit in. As if I was supposed to grow up—get married—have children—work outside the home—and wait for retirement to sit back and live through my grandchildren! But it is just like you said, Astro— those were my perceptions, and I know that none of these folks were really out to get me—it just felt like it at the time.

Astro: *(responding from personal experience)* A common mistake, my friend. So, how do your shelves look now?

The Being: *(looking around in amazement)* Well, quite frankly, it's a bit of a mess in here, as video cans are kind of strewn everywhere

... and the shredding machine is still hacking up my last few items, at least the ones I can see.

I imagine there are plenty more cans, but not on my conscious level. In any event, didn't I hear you say we will be dissolving the whole room?

Astro: *(fully confident)* Indeed you did, and if you are ready, we will proceed.

The Being: *(pondering)* Okay, now what?

Astro: *(returning inward, with eyes closed once again)* To dissolve all of the energy that has been on a repetitious basis within our awareness, I'd like you now to look *behind* the shredding machine and pull out a huge box filled with pineapple-sized grenades. Now, these are very special grenades, for, just like sparklers, once these grenades explode, they use colored, vibrating energy to absorb all the video cans, shelving, shredding machine, and bin. They are also time-released with a ten-minute delay, thus giving you time to get downstairs, out the front door, and away from the building—and giving you a front row view of all the energy exploding right out through the side of the building, where it dissolves into nothingness.

(brief pause)

Astro: *(watching intently)* Are you ready, Being? If so, begin to pull the pins, placing lots of grenades around the room, especially in the corners and into the back of the room, and let me know when you have them all in place.

The Being: *(full of energy, scurrying around the room, dropping grenades every few feet)* Just a moment more. Okay, all pins pulled and ready to go!

Astro: *(quick to reply)* Okay, hurry out of the room, being sure to secure the door, and run to the elevators, taking the one that is waiting to return you to the lobby. Once you reach the lobby, leave quickly through the glass doors, go down the cement stairs, and quickly move around to the side of the building. It's getting close . . . 5 . . . 4 . . . 3 . . . 2 . . . 1 . . . BAVOOM!!!

The Being: *(marveling at the sight)* Wow! Would you look at that! There is a huge hole there on the third floor where a wall used to be! And yet, the rest of the building is intact. It's some kind of miracle, I'm sure!

Astro: *(full of wonder as well)* Yes, you might call the imaginative nature some kind of miracle! But we aren't finished yet. Now that you have the space cleared out, I'd like you to consider just exactly what you want to use that space for now, to support you and your employees. For example, some people enjoy nature and put mountains and streams, birds, trees, and so on for all of their employees to enjoy during the day. Then others like a type of health club, complete with juice bar, massage, body-building machines, and such. For some, it's a day care center where all of the employees who have children can have them nearby. And again, please remember that this area is designed purely to match *your* needs, no one else's. Remember, your employees are here solely to serve you.

So, what would you like?

The Being: *(jumping up and down enthusiastically)* I can see it already. Since I seem to have lots of energy, I would love to have a forest of redwood trees that has a clearing where a beautiful lake with grassy shores is perfect for swimming. And I want this forest full of animal friends and magical creatures like elves and unicorns. And then I want to have plenty of wildflowers in the forest, nurtured by the sun shining through the trees. This way, I and my members will be able to enjoy the peace and serenity of the forest and swim to my heart's content. And of course, all of my employees could come and go as they please and not have to run into anyone if they so chose.

Astro: *(chuckling out loud)* I can tell by your quick reply that you like your new creation. I have to admit, I like it too. It feels so open and, with the wall gone, you are not limited in any way.

By the way, do you recall if your Video Library was on the left or right side of the corridor?

The Being: *(with no hesitation)* Yes, I do. The door was on the left. Why do you ask?

Astro: *(not surprised by the response)* Because it often is an indication of whether you are Mentally or Emotionally based. In this case, the left door relates to the Emotional nature, and the right side of the corridor to the Mental base. However, we will find out with more certainty about your vantage point as we complete the Board Room process. So, if you are ready, we can proceed.

(The Being now realizes that It had felt a little apprehensive when Astro first requested that It let go of Its images of Its members and not to use any predetermined notions—not knowing what to expect. But now the Being begins to feel the anxious-ness receding, and in its place, hope and possibilities beginning to filter in.)

I'd rather be seen for who I am and be alone,
than be accepted for someone I'm not and be lonely.

—Brock Tully, *Reflections for Someone Special*

Whether I'm right, whether I'm wrong,
Whether I find a place in the world or never belong,
I've got to be Me, I've got to be Me,
Daring to try, to do it or die—
I've got to be me.

—Sammy Davis, Jr.

Have it, enjoy it, and let go and move along into the next stage.

—National Velvet

♡ CHAPTER SEVEN ♡

THE OFFICIAL BOARD ROOM

(In Its mind's eye, the Being slowly begins to walk back toward the entrance to Its private skyscraper, marveling at the newly-created landscape where the video library had previously been.)

Astro: *(glad to assist, but beginning to tire)* To continue, I'd like to ask you to re-enter your building, climb the cement stairs, and go in through the glass doors to the lobby of your building.

166

This time, instead of taking one of the several elevators to your left, we will be taking the lone elevator to your right, which goes *only* to the top floor. Once we are inside the elevator and the button is pushed, it will take a moment or two for us to reach the very top. So, while we are in motion, I would like to tell you a little bit about what we will find once we arrive at the top floor.

(the Being makes Its way to the elevator, entering and pressing the only button on the panel as the elevator starts its ascent)

First of all, we will step out into a small reception area. There may be one or two desks in this area, which may or may not have someone seated at them. To the right of this area is a long hallway that leads to two huge oak doors. On the other side of those doors is your Board Room. I will tell you now that once we enter the Board Room, we will be looking for your Board members—the Physical body representative, the Mental body representative, and the Emotional body representative, who may or may not be in the room. As you well know, they may or may not make their appearance in human form.

So now, the elevator is beginning to slow down, and finally it comes to a halt. As you step out into the reception area, is there anyone seated at the desk or desks? Again, there is no right or wrong answer, only what *you* see with your internal vision. Then, with each piece of information you share, the more we know about your particular situation and point of view.

The Being: *(viewing an internal scene)* Well . . . the first thing I notice about the space is all of the plants. Some are in large pots and others are sitting on the two desks in the reception area. And now I see that someone is at one of the desks, and the other person is watering the plants.

Astro: *(continuing from some inner strength, rather than from rest)* Thank you, Being, for giving me all of the information that you are receiving. If indeed there had not been someone in the reception area, it would merely have meant that we were meeting on a weekend or holiday, enabling you to have full privacy. As it is, you, like most Emotionally-based Beings, are not embarrassed or disturbed by others' presence when unfolding something that matters to you—as long as you are feeling safety in the space provided.

(after a brief pause) Now, if you would, I'd like you to walk down the hall on your way to the two large oak doors and look under your feet to see what color the carpet is there. What does your imagination tell you?

The Being: *(quite taken with Itself)* Oh . . . it's a beautiful mauve color . . . sort of a pinkish-purplish blend.

Astro: *(regaining some of its resiliency)* Just keep that information at hand, as we reach the oak doors. Now, before we actually enter the Board Room, I want to let you know that, for purposes of orienting ourselves in terms of direction, we will say that these oak doors are in the south, and that the north will be in front of us as we enter the room. So, as we pass through the doors into the Board Room, the right side of the room is towards the east, and the left side is west. So now, open the double doors and step into the room.

Look around and get a feel for it, checking in all directions. I would like you to tell me now if the room feels enclosed and cozy, or open and expansive.

The Being: *(taking a moment to fully note the room's dimensions and feel)* It's not huge, but it feels quite spacious.

Astro: *(really getting into the scenario, now)* Okay . . . now look around and see if there are any windows, skylights, or other openings or light sources—or if the lights are out.

The Being: *(in all honesty)* At first I really didn't see the room. I only felt it. But now I'm seeing light flooding into the room from the window panes that cover the whole north wall and from smaller ones to the east, and I can gauge the size of the room to be about twenty feet tall, with a ceiling that is more of a cloud cover than anything solid. The length of the room is impressive as well, reaching twice as far as its height. On the west wall is light-colored wood paneling, with a painting of some sort, which I can't seem to see clearly right now. And then the east wall is rather plain; it's painted off-white with an unusually-shaped window, with a pane shaped like a star in its center, amidst smaller panes of glass.

Astro: *(in a quiet voice)* Do you notice anything particular about the lightness or heaviness of your Board Room?

The Being: *(pondering this)* Yeah . . . you know, it looks like the north and the east are more cloud-like, harder to see. Does that mean anything?

Astro: *(focusing on all of the details)* Indeed it does. But for today, though, I would like to gather more information before I divulge any more meaning. In any case, I would not like you to think that I planted these notions in your awareness. After all, this is your Board Room, not mine. Given the same suggested imagery, I would come up with an entirely differ-ent picture. And, speaking of pictures, can you get closer to your west wall? See if the painting comes into your conscious view.

The Being: *(tentatively)* I'll try. . . . Why, it's the forest I created on the third floor, and the beautiful lake with the grassy shore! How did it get up here, when I created it only moments ago in the Video Library room?

Astro: *(quite taken with the Being's unfoldment)* What you believe to have created so recently was actually with you on the subconscious level all of the time. It took merely removing all of the debris that had been placed over it, to locate it within you. That's why we visit the Video Library first, to free up aspects of the Self that are with us, just not on the conscious level.

Now, at this time, I'd like you to look down toward the floor and see what color the carpet is now inside your Board Room. Or, perhaps it is no longer carpet, but hardwood flooring or perhaps marble. What do you see, Being?

The Being: *(ecstatic)* Wow! Here the carpet is a brilliant, emerald green! And, it's even more plush than the mauve.

Astro: *(fondly)* I'm glad you like it—now I can give you some more information about your Self. Since the areas are both covered with carpet, it indicates that you have mostly felt that you have been on your path in life and also that, for reasons of your own, you generally choose to present a different picture to the world at large than you do to the people who are closest to you. Many of us recognize that it isn't always safe or appreciated to fully Self-express, so what we share with others is often vague or general, if not out-right misdirected, so as to protect the Self. If indeed the flooring had changed to hardwood, marble, or whatever, inside the Board Room itself, it might show that indeed you have experienced along your life's path a significant change in your perception, that a decision has been made to view circumstances differently. Or, it could mean that, due to fear, you paint a totally separate picture of yourself for the benefit of others and sometimes to fool the Self, losing track of your particular direction and focus.

I'd like to ask you now to check the shape of your room. For some, it appears to be a traditional square or rectangle, while others find themselves inside a more unique configuration. So, where do you place yourself in reference to the shape of your Board Room?

The Being: *(not knowing quite what to think)* Well, I suppose I'm somewhere in between. It basically has the four directions; however, each side has two parts, as though the side of the wall comes to a outward-directed point in the middle, giving the room an octagonal appearance, except for the flat, south side, where the oak doors are located.

Astro: *(fascinated)* How interesting! This facet deals with your desire to follow rules or not. I'd say you sort of follow them, but not to the point that they get in the way of your desire to experience life fully.

(the Being nods Its agreement)

Astro: *(continuing internally to scan the board room)* Now for room amenities. Are there any plants, pictures—other than the one you mentioned earlier, furniture, or anything else that you noticed?

The Being: *(seeing clearly)* Oh, yes. It's full of lush plants, some in huge pots and others hanging off metal brackets attached to the walls on the west and the east. Plus, there is a side unit, like a wet bar, full of juices, fresh water, and herbal teas. And, in the center of the room is a large rectangular table with twelve chairs, six on each side, with a larger chair at the head of the table, facing the oak doors. I believe the table is made of mahogany.

Astro: *(with growing respect)* Boy, you really are getting good at this imagination business. So, let me share a little bit more about you, from the information you have provided. First of all, before I forget, the difference in your feel regarding the solidarity to the west versus the cloud-like vagueness to the north and east indicates that you have more fullness and certainty in your Emotional nature. What this means is, the Mental and Physical natures are not as solidly connected to you as the Emotional member, and therefore their information and experiences come to you, the Being, like static electricity. In addition, you are definitely not interested in Normal; you like variety, adventure, and natural phenomena. And, by the size, shape, and color of your conference table, it appears that the idea of responsibility weighs heavily upon you at times.

Also, the fact that there are more than three chairs at the table—for we all have a three-member Board of Directors to enable us to handle third-dimensional living—indicates that several people in your experience really do believe they have a greater say in your life than you do, especially one person.

The Being: *(bubbling over with glee)* You've got that right! It's as though my desire to play in life must be tempered with serious responsibilities—and I fight it all the way. I have to admit, it poops me out sometimes. I sense the person sitting at the head of my table is myself as I've been told I should be, rather than the constantly unfolding, sometimes embarrassing, but always playful person I know myself to be.

Astro: *(wanting to help)* Well, if you like, Being, we can alter this duality of Self here today, but before we do, I'd like you to check and see if any of your members are in the room right now.

(The Being looks around and is surprised to find the room empty. After all, up until a short while earlier, It had been surrounded by Jaguar, Wizard and Deer . . . and a feeling of dread begins to form in Its stomach . . . .)

Astro: *(watching the Being's enthusiasm start to waver)* I bet you're wondering where your earlier visions of these members went.

(the Being nods tentatively)

Astro: *(encouragingly)* Well, do keep in mind you are a little ahead of most folks, who don't even have a clue as to how their three densest bodies look or are currently operating. For them, just being able to *locate* their members is a task in itself. And, from the point of view of the Board members, after all, if this were the first time since arriving on the planet that someone had asked to meet with you, well, you might be a little curious as to why *now*, after such a long silence. Would *you* just show up as if nothing had happened? Of course not. And if the idea upsets *you*, just image what your members might think of it! Remember, up until now, they thought they were in charge of you, instead of the other way around. So, you might have to give them a little encouragement to show up, and not just via an interoffice memo. For example, I would have to ask you to think about how you view yourself physically in order to get the Physical member to show up. So, you would need to look to see if you exercise, have energy, carry extra weight, fidget nervously, and so on, in order to paint an image of your Physical body member.

Then, mentally, you'd have to ask yourself if you consider your Self to be smart, quick, untechnical, practical, orderly, and so on, or not. Whether these considerations are true or not, we do hold ourselves a certain way in our own internal mirror. The image you create will reflect these notions.

On the other front, emotionally, you'd have to look and see if you had emoted recently or not, and check on such nebulous items as flow or blockage, vitality or lethargy, joy or repression, and the like. These items are usually not so hard to locate, once you start looking. After all, you, Being, were easily able to create visions of your members, with Jaguar's help. Had you not had this opportunity and didn't know from personal experience what I was talking about, you might still be looking for your members' creative images.

Let me remind you that these images do not always represent something familiar, practical, or likable to us, at least not at first. I've known some Beings to come up with such members as an old rag, a huge boulder, and broken glass. The important factor is to accept and work with whoever or whatever shows up—for we are dealing with matters of self-worth here, and the beginning of some major cellular memory changes that can work towards unblocking our ability to manifest clear, natural, abundant flow in our lives.

(with emphatic certainty) I'd like you to realize, Being, that *not* having your members show up is perfect for you right now. The key factor is to get *present*—to allow them to

appear to you in their most present images. You see, any time we can get *present with our Selves*, we have the opportunity to grow and change. So, I want you to know that your members are not gone, but rather that they are in transition and haven't yet come fully into your new vision. When their new forms appear, their contributions to you as a whole Being will be such that each will be able to access and share you— and your entire universe of conscious awareness—*as one*.

But for now, since your members are not present, Being, I'm going to ask you to remove the heavy table and all of the chairs, just for today. You may want to leave them in the hall or take them to another room off the nearby reception area. In any event, I'd like to ask you to bring in an equilateral, triangular table, constructed of any material you like, but with rounded corners. Place this table in the center of the room, orienting one rounded corner to the north, one to the east, and another to the west, which leaves a flat side of the table to the south where the oak doors are located. So, if you are facing the table from the flat, south side, you have a corner to your left, one to your right, and one straight across the table from you.

Now, at this point I'd like you to put three identical, comfort-able chairs around the table, one at each corner. If your members were already present in the room, I would have you ask them now to take a seat. However, in your case, we will have to invite them in before we can proceed. I remind you that these body representatives may take just about any kind of appearance: they may look like some aspect of nature, a version of you, an animal, a light or geometric figure, or perhaps an inanimate object. The possibilities are endless.

So, let's start with the Physical body representative. Take a look at your Self from a physical standpoint, and see if any image comes forth which appears to be related to you on a physical level.

The Being: *(pondering out loud Its physical self-perception)* Let me see . . . I *so* liked that beautiful, big cat, but for some reason I don't currently feel as light and agile as a Jaguar. So—how do I feel, physically? . . . Hmmmm . . . a bit tired, uncertain, and heavy even. Oh, my. *(slightly dismayed)* I see a giant oak tree.

Astro: *(answering before the Being can retreat)* Great! Don't try to figure it out. Just have it take a seat at the table, and continue to let your creative juices flow. Now, how about the Mental member? Look to see what you are thinking, and how supportive or not it seems to you as a total Being. Also look to see how you view yourself along intellectual lines.

(in no time at all, the Being envisions a pool of muddy water and feels even more gloom set in)

The Being: *(in upset)* I see muddy water . . . and I don't like it.

Astro: *(trying to soothe)* Well, well, well. Not so easy to keep judgment at bay, is it? But don't worry, the process is not over yet. Just be sure this member in its current form takes a seat. Okay, now let's issue the invitation for the Emotional body representative to join us today. Remember, it doesn't matter what mood you are in; the image will come to you as you focus on your feelings.

The Being: *(hopeful)* I do see a beam of light. Well, actually, it is a moving, pulsating light, with little sparkles of color that glimmer as it moves. *(slightly awestruck)* . . . It's quite beautiful!

Astro: *(with a sense of revelation)* A little different than the Mental member, don't you agree?

The Being: *(more energized)* Oh, yes! But how can one member appear so different from another?

Astro: *(happy to reply)* For one thing, their duties are entirely different, and the key factor is whether they are free to do their job—or if they have to spend a great portion of their energy guarding some aspect of your Self. Now look to see who sat down in which seats.

The Being: *(desperately wanting to do the process "right")* Well, the Physical image, the oak tree, sat in the east; the Mental or muddy water took the north corner, and the light beam, the Emotional representative, floated over to the west.

Astro: *(in acknowledgment)* Very good. However, each member *is* in charge of its own area and has its own specific chair. In your case, the Emotional member is the only one in its own chair. Has it, by any chance, had some recent opportunities to clear your feelings?

The Being: *(with curiosity)* Why, yes, as you know, it was during our discussion earlier in the day—but why?

Astro: *(stating quite simply)* Because your Emotional member is demonstrating that it is currently in its area of jurisdiction by having seated itself in its own correct vantage point for viewing the whole person that you are.

Remember earlier, when the north and east areas of the room seemed clouded and harder to see? Well, you were picking up this disparity amongst the Board members regarding their own areas of jurisdiction. For, as pointed out earlier, the

Mental member is *never* in the moment, and, conversely, the Emotional and Physical representatives are *always* in the moment.

Whenever they are seated in each other's chairs, the result is confusion and a drain on your physical vitality. So please ask the Physical and Mental team players to stand up and change chairs. Now don't be surprised if the Mental member is a bit miffed, because, as in most Board rooms, THE chairperson sits opposite the doors leading into the room. And, quite often the Mental nature takes on the notion that it is in charge of the Physical and Emotional members, rather than the fact that it is one of three equal but diverse partners.

So now I would have you, the Essence, stand behind each member in turn, and ask whether that member can support the other two with full admiration and respect. If not, we will need to make some changes.

(as the Being, in Its mind's eye, moves to stand behind the brilliant, vibrating light—already knowing that It feels unhappy with the other members—It receives confirmation of this disparity from the pulsating light . . . .)

Astro: *(probing gently)* So, what are you seeing, Emotional member?

Light Beam: *(all aglow)* Just what the Being envisioned. The Physical is strong, but it seems so rigid and overbearing—and the Mental is so depressing. I'd rather work alone than with these two.

Astro: *(getting the message)* Okay, thank you. And now, Being, move on over to your Physical body representative and stand behind it, so you can view the members from its position. What is your view, O mighty Oak Tree?

Oak Tree: *(answering solidly)* I'm drawn to the light, but its brightness is almost blinding, as though it is somehow better than me. And, although the muddy water would be soothing to my roots, I don't believe that I am seeing the Mental member at its full potential.

Astro: *(simply receiving the communication)* Thank you, Physical image. Now, how about you—the Mental body representative? Go stand behind it, Being, and let your Self see through its eyes.

Muddy Water: *(full of judgment)* Well, all I can say is that this is a sorry lot, and I'm not about to support anything that can't seem to find a nice thing to say about me. I'm just not going to work that hard! Remember, you two, I live outside the moment— which is *all* in my domain—and if you two go and mess up the moment of experience, then you will just have to clean up your own mess! So there!

Astro: *(taken aback)* My, my, my! It seems you have opened a real can of worms here.

(the Being, in shock, finds Itself unable to utter any words)

Astro: *(regaining its composure)* The good news is, Being, that we are not yet done with this process. And please appreciate that this is a necessary step, for in order to grasp your Self fully, you must get fully into the experience of separate-ness that each of your members is feeling, at this time in your life, to see just how difficult it is currently for you to manifest what you want. You might say your internal filters are clogged, and therefore your desires don't get met.

Have you noticed yet that all of this discord is completely within you? We haven't even branched out and talked to anyone from the outside yet who might be exerting influence or pulls over you.

Perhaps you are beginning to see that the manner in which each of us operates within our own Physical form, with our own thoughts and feelings, definitely affects our interpretation of the world around us. In your case, right now, your filters are indicating rigidity, confusion, the notion of being "better than," and hostility. Sort of makes it hard to be fully present in the moment, doesn't it?

(the Being, still in shock, only nods)

Astro: *(encouragingly)* Well, let's move on and try to clear up things as we go. To start with, I have yet to mention that there is a door flush with the wall over to the right side of the large, oak doors. To open this door, just push in on it, and you will see that it is like a dressing room inside. We are now going to ask each member, individually, to step inside and seek to uncover its most accurate vision of itself in its full potential, according to you.

A man cannot step in the same river twice.

—Heraclitus

♡ The Changing Room ♡

Astro: *(matter-of-factly)* So, who do you want to start with?

The Being: *(barely muttering)* Let's go with the Mental member.

Astro: *(straining to hear the Being's response)* Okay, but be sure to thank the member for showing up before it steps into the changing room.

(the Being gives the Muddy Water a subdued "thank you for coming," while escorting it into the small side room)

Astro: *(sounding quite professional)* Now, I believe that earlier your Physical body representative described to you some of the attributes of these members—back when you were trying to describe your Self—and these were amazingly accurate. So, if I sound repetitious to you, please forgive me. But—like the stream within whose course you can never step twice in the same water, for the water is always moving—you are not the same Being you were when you began describing yourself! So, even though the information might be the same, you will quite likely hear the information differently. I remind you to *be present* and accept what *currently* presents itself to you. Both you and each of your members will know if its individual description seems right or not.

(addressing the Mental member) So, Mental body representative, while you are in the changing room, I will describe for your Being your many attributes and contributions to Its

181

experience of living. First of all, as you are well aware, you are never in the moment. Your domain is the past and the future, and you have the ability to go way into the past and way into the future, or to the immediate past or future. Therefore, you hold the thin, silver, connecting cord of continuity for the Being to be able to see what lessons it has learned, which ones it is currently learning, and which ones it has yet to learn. You enable the Being to remember who it loves, where it is going, and what it is interested in, as well as to hold future dreams and visions. If you focus solely on the past, you can harbor resentment and anger, as well as fond memories. At the same time, if you concern yourself only with tomorrow, the riches of yesterday's experiences are lost to your Being. You store all information and data, which results in a wealth of knowledge.

Therefore, all created ideas and the ability literally to "make up your world" to match your standards and integrity, begin in the Mental member's jurisdiction. You can even analyze and figure out, but *you are not here to judge*. For all judging, criticizing, negating, and limiting either your "Self" or another, is actually running your Feelings or Physicality through the Mental doorway. And, how could you judge, if it is also within your jurisdiction to back the Being and the other two members of your Self-expression team one hundred percent—and I mean *one hundred percent*—of the time? In addition, you house one of the two healers that are given to each Essence when it comes into a physical form, and that is the gift of forgiveness. Just like movie film, once an item or someone is given your full forgiveness—and not just lip service, or "I can forgive this, but I can't forget it!"—said item automatically becomes deleted from your personal internal records—and you are no longer affected by it or react to anything related to it. With all of this in mind, Being, how do you see your Mental body team player now?

(the Being pauses and lets the information play over and over in Its consciousness, knowing that while the data seeps in, the Mental body member is undergoing a metamorphosis inside the changing room. . . . and finally, the Being responds . . .)

The Being: *(feeling more bouyant)* I can see my Mental counterpart now: it's so clear and sparkling! It is a large Amethyst Crystal. Not just clear stone, but a deep, beautiful purple that radiates such clarity and certainty. Wow, I feel so drawn to it. I don't see any rough edges to snag me, either, or any hostility. I mean, it just *is*, and it seems to be energizing within itself, like a flow. It seems crazy to say, but I feel as though it is moving and changing inside, like it's alive. I never thought about the aliveness of crystals before, but obviously they do grow.

(as the Being directs more of Its attention toward the stone, it seems to pulsate even more strongly)

The Being: *(totally in awe, to Astro)* I am *really* impressed. I have to admit I was very concerned when the images first presented themselves, especially when you mentioned the fact that this member is supposed to be one hundred percent behind the rest of us. I mean to say, I was pretty skeptical. . . . to my knowledge, the only thing I know of that operates one hundred percent of the time is gravity. Wow, to think I can be supported one hundred percent—*one hundred percent* of the time!—especially by something so beautiful, powerful, and brilliant—sounds so wonderful. What a miracle. And I don't have to manipulate another person—or short myself—to get this support! . . .

Astro: *(cutting in)* Wait one minute, Being. Before you get carried away with this idea, let me mention that the Mental nature will experience a lag time between this realization on the part of your Essence and its manifestation in the three-dimensional world. What I mean to say is, it will be a good four to six weeks before this new, conscious awareness becomes fully integrated and operational in the Mental body's domain. In the meantime, your old habit energies are going to try real hard to get you to return to old and familiar ways. For example, a woman may hate to get beaten on a regular basis by her husband, but at least it is familiar. In such an uncertain world, many Beings prefer some regularity, even unhealthy regularity, over a multitude of unknowns. So don't get on your own case for the next month or two. However, if you do notice undesired habitual action taking over, remind yourself of the changes that you have made internally—and of your desire to see these changes externally. In Mental terms, this relates to positive affirmations, i.e., new videos, such as: *I AM AN INCREDIBLE, MAGNIFICENT, PRICELESS GIFT* and *I AM A GOOD PERSON WHO DOES HAVE WORTH-WHILE THINGS TO SHARE, NATURALLY.*

In addition, you will quite likely need to acknowledge any judgment, criticism, negativity, and limitation that you hear inside your own head about yourself or any other Being—or from someone else. One way to do this is to say, "Thank you, Mind, for sharing that information with me," or "I really appreciate you bringing that to my attention." As with all minds, who work very hard to do their best for each of us, it just wants to be appreciated for all its efforts on your behalf—and be sure to take a moment to really, sincerely, find something to thank the Mind or that other person for—again, bearing in mind that tone of voice is determined by the Emotional nature, and we can all tell when we are being flippant in our speech.

I can assure you that, sometime in the next four-to-six-week period, your desired new ways of expressing will surface on their own. After all, the Mental body representative has to know if you mean it. Otherwise, we wouldn't have any continuity to rely on, or any way to gauge our internal spiritual growth. Besides, the Mental member has a huge good-idea basket within the Physical form. I mean, if we tried to accomplish everything we thought of, we'd never get done in this lifetime. So, we all create lots of thoughts that never leave the drawing board, so to speak, and end up in the eternal good-idea basket. For, you see, thought recognizes that it generates within its own realm. If we were to stop to handle every thought that deals with items unrelated to our particular life's story, we would get side-tracked from our purpose, natural talents, and accomplishments. So it is important to be able to filter out the ideas we create and the ideas given to us by others that don't relate to our main path in life, or that don't lead where natural abundant flow exists for us. For example, an unhappy young man—who became an attorney because his father was one, and because the father wanted his son to join him in the family firm—may find his love of outdoors nurtured by becoming a forest ranger. To say we all want to do the same things and live the same life is ludicrous, and besides, as you may have noticed, Being, people do thrive on a certain amount of variety.

The Being: (*with more vocal thrust*) Indeed we do. I've just always had so much fear that it made even the fun experiences a problem.

But something is different now, and I think I know what it is. I've never had the full support of my Mental member before. It was so busy trying to protect me that I felt in the lurch and would withdraw myself into an illusion of separation and disconnectedness. And then, I'd be off and running in full reaction to everything. What a vicious cycle. I'll be glad to let that one go.

Astro: *(inquiring)* Would you like to continue this process with another of your members?

The Being: *(more sure of Itself)* Indeed I would—particularly the Physical body member.

Astro: *(feeling the surge of energy from the Being)* Okay, be sure to thank it for coming, and give it a huge hug before placing it in the changing room.

(the Being wraps both of its hints-of-arms around the trunk of the oak tree in a grateful bear hug and then escorts it into the changing room)

Astro: *(nodding approvingly)* Now I will state the Physical team member's attributes, just as this member did for you at the beginning of this story.

The Physical body representative is not only a member of your Self-expressing team, but it is a witness to all that goes on in your life. It stores each life experience, whether deemed high or low, good or bad, routine or exceptional, in its body parts. It even stores the Mental and Emotional memories of these experiences as well, which explains our reactive responses to certain stimuli. For example, if someone comes up behind you and says a big *Hello!*—you go through the roof, because the surprise of it startles you—and the whole incident reminds you of the time you got off a horse, turned your back to it, and got scared when it shoved its nose into your back—all of this having occurred when you were only ten years old. And, to top it off, at the time, one of your friends laughed at you for getting scared over a gentle horse, so you couldn't let out all of the fear that you in fact felt. Therefore, that same unexpressed fear gets triggered whenever you get taken by surprise.

Being the densest system in which we operate, the Physical body truly has the final say as to our health and vitality. We've all been in that situation where we were going along in life and WHAM! our stomach acts up, or we trip and fall and twist our ankle. In those moments, all of our attention goes to the Physical form. In the more extreme cases of heart attack or cancer, our attention is full of our physical discomfort, and pain becomes the center of our daily focus. Or, in periods of Mental or Emotional stress, the Physical body may "contribute" a state of ill-ness as a gesture of Self-protection, not only as a means of distracting the Mental and Emotional focus from other concerns, but also because as long as the Being is listed on the injured reserve, It is far less likely to come under direct attack.

In addition, the Physical representative is in charge of three specific areas of jurisdiction. They are strength, both inner and outer; flexibility; and trust, both of ourselves and others. Strength is pretty obvious externally, for we can see whether we have stamina or not, or whether lifting a package is too much strain for us. On the other hand, internal strength—often known as strength of character—is not so easy to see. This entails commitment, integrity, and purpose, which are not subjects we learn about in school. They are abstractual and interpreted by each of us in our own way. And, just to keep things interesting, they are not stationary but constantly moving and growing.

Flexibility is also a double-edged sword. It not only refers to being physically limber, but also mentally and emotionally fluid, the ability to be able to flow with life's circumstances as well as life's opportunities. It may sound easy on paper, but just ask anyone if living these attributes is as easy as thinking about them. Most often the answer is no.

Finally, this member deals with trust. Now *there* is an elusive fellow. Just exactly what is trust? And how does one determine its existence? These are questions we are all engaged in. For our purposes here today, I would like to say trust is the state of knowing-ness that just seems right on line. It doesn't concern itself with physical evidence, but rather seems to relate to a flow of effortless living. That definition even sounds vague to me. But I hope, Being, that you are getting a sense of this team player, rather than an exact picture of *my* interpretation of trust. For this one, you must look deep within your Self, to see the magnitude of this element of Physical body jurisdiction, as it relates to you.

So give your Self as Essence a moment to digest all this information, and allow your member to complete its transformation in the changing room.

(The Being takes Astro's advice and sits with this data, imagining the information as filtering down through all Its pores into Its individual body parts before finally reaching the Being Itself. And at that moment the Being speaks . . . .)

The Being: *(extremely embarrassed)* First of all, I want to say that I have never really given my Physical form much consideration. I guess you could say I've taken it for granted. Over the years, I never really considered it such a vital part of my experiencing my Self in form. For that I am sorry, because I never realized all that it does on my behalf—and for the most part without complaint. So, before my Physical member emerges from the changing room, I want to apologize for my lack of awareness and also to thank it for all that it has done for me.

Astro: *(quite astonished)* Well said! I do believe you will see quite a difference in this member once it emerges from the dressing room, for gratitude provides such a great energy boost to all life forms. So now, ask your member to step out and show you its image.

The Being: *(feeling stronger)* Okay. Physical body representative, please show me your reflection.

(as the Being speaks, the door opens and out steps the most beautiful and gentle Unicorn, with its horn glowing . . . .)

The Being: *(speechless with awe)* WOW!

(stepping closer to the gorgeous white horse with the illuminated horn) You are so magical!

Unicorn: *(shimmering in radiant light)* Thanks to you. For it was you who changed me from an ordinary horse into the magical creature you see before you. It was your willingness to let go of your earthly concerns and expand your gratitude that enabled me to make this transformation. Although I appear to be the densest member, the opposite is also true. The whole universe—at least from your perception—exists within me. I am the culmination of nothing and everything, and it is my job to see that there is room for growth and change at every moment, allowing for the richest possible experience in form.

(with that comment, the Unicorn takes its seat in the North, noticing the brilliant, pulsating, purple glow of the Amethyst Crystal in the East and nodding its approval . . .)

Astro: *(thrilled at the results so far)* Since we've transformed your Mental and Physical body representatives, there is only one more to work with—the Emotional member. So, please ask it to go into the changing room, after you give it a big hug, and thank it also for showing up.

(the Being happily hugs the brilliant beam of white light and, thanking it for coming forward today, sends it into the changing room)

Astro: *(proceeding with the final member's transformation)* So now let me give you the attributes of this body representative. Just like the Physical member, the Emotional body is always in the moment. What I mean by that is, this member houses the cleansers: laughter, anger, sadness, and so on. And remember, people do not plan to laugh at exactly three minutes from now; rather, it just comes up in the moment that it does. And when we are upset with ourselves or others, we are mad when we are mad, and not a moment sooner or later. In the case of sadness, we don't turn it on or off, even though we do try to hide it at times. We remain sad until the moment we realize we are no longer sad.

Now, before I go further, I wish to comment on fear. Most people would call this an emotion, and we definitely do feel its presence. However, I've noticed that fear is actually a moment of uncertainty that the Mental nature runs with—as someone once put it, F.E.A.R., for False Events Appearing Real. More aptly put, fear of the unknown falls in the Mental's realm, because this is the only foundation member who does not experience the moment, where all knowingness lies—and, as I've mentioned before, this member looks outside itself to determine its responses. So, once it activates a moment of doubt, many times the Emotional system receives the thought as truth and reacts accordingly. Rousseau described this phenomenon aptly by observing, "My life has been a series of terrible calamities, most of which never even happened to me!"

While I'm on this subject of items that originate in one member's arena but get blown out of proportion in another's jurisdiction, I'd like to mention willfulness. Willfulness is also a brief thought that the Emotional system blows out of proportion. Even though the original idea came from the Mental's realm, it is the Emotional member who forces the issue. In willfulness, or trying to force the issue rather than flowing naturally, all energies are focused on lack of faith and trust in the greater Self's ability to orchestrate all vibration and energy. Then, "for-me-to-win-you-have-to-lose" rules the day. In either case, both members are out of balance, and the result tends to be some sort of catastrophe, often to the Physical form.

To get back purely to the Emotional body, this member's main attribute is in the area of connection. The Emotional body connects created thought in the Mental's jurisdiction to physical manifestation in the Physical body's arena, by providing the interest or *oomph!* to follow through so the idea can become visible in the world. For example, a company that focuses only on the number of products sold or projected income and profit and loss statements or other facts and figures, and that does not put equal concern into the quality of working conditions or to the employees assembling the products, will often find itself with labor disputes and discord within the company. At the same time, a company that sees to the whole scope of producing their product, including working conditions, ecological impact, and individual needs like day care, will tend, within the larger scope of things, to find their profit margins soaring with fewer disruptions.

The same is true within a family. When a parent comes home late from work after the boss has yelled at them, they are tired and upset, and their ability to be fully present and excited for their children wanes, so they snap at their kids. With enough such occurrences, the children can interpret this as their not having any importance or worth, and a gap begins to form between them and the parent. On the other hand, we have all been in that position of being tossed around in life and wanting to lash out at difficult circumstances, but it is still possible to let it out by hollering or singing in the car, and even to tell your children your truth as it appears to you. In so doing, it is possible that you might become more real to them and bridge the so-called gap of generations that appears to exist between parents and children. After all, children, like ourselves, simply wish to be heard. I'm not saying this is easy by any means—just possible. And it is the Emotional system that determines the difference. This is the one body in most of us who has been the least developed and who grows only in the moment of the upset or concern.

This body member houses Wisdom, that which "knows what it knows," not what it has learned, as in the Mental member's case. This is also called "knowing-ness" and extends to "intuition." We all know when we have been touched with kindness and when we have not. As U.S. Supreme Court

Justice Oliver Wendell Holmes once said, "Even a dog distin-
guishes the difference between being stumbled over and
being kicked." Even before we could formulate sentences, we
could tell things from the tone of someone's voice. For
example, if anyone has ever shouted "I LOVE YOU!" or any
other statement with acid venom in their voice to you, you
understand what I mean. As far as the words go, it may be a
wonderful sentiment. But the tone says, "You worthless piece
of garbage," or "What is the matter with you, anyway!" And
I've also heard a phrase once which says, "Words are cheap."
So, which message do you think you'd follow, Being?

The Being: *(without forethought)* It's evident to me whenever a person is
angry with me, no matter what words they use. And more to
the point, I know I'd get very nervous at such a mixed
message and would probably start shutting down to that
person.

Astro: *(nodding its approval)* A common assessment. At that point,
quite often you'd find two people withholding both trust and
safety, which the Physical body determines. And then, before
long, loving touch goes right out the window.

The Being: *(pondering the matter)* What I don't understand is why a
person wouldn't notice that they are sending a mixed message.

Astro: *(quite taken with the thought)* That's a good question, and it
has to do with the bases about which I spoke to you earlier. A
Mentally-based being, one who makes changes once it under-
stands something, generally speaking doesn't listen for the
touch or tone of its words. It considers *the words and their
meaning* as the crux of any communication, focusing on the

preciseness of each word exchanged. The Emotionally-based being, on the other hand, listens more to *the flow and the sound of the words*, and, when speaking, concerns itself mainly *with the feeling or general idea* it is trying to convey. Only secondarily does it notice *what* was said. This nature expresses in the moment, so these people tend to be more acutely aware of when someone is present with them, and also when they are not. Quite efffortlessly, they respond by giving the other their full attention and also naturally seek to receive full attention from their present company. At the same time, this ability to focus full attention on whatever they are thinking about, can sometimes lead to being absent-minded of other thoughts. It's quite common for an Emotionally-based human Being to be listening to someone and midway through the conversation focus on an entirely different situation, only to pick up the thread of the conversation at the end, and reply, "Sure I heard you," and merely fill in the gaps from their own life experiences, which is a form of assumption. Unfortunately, what they fill in the gaps with may have nothing to do with the speaker's comments or requests.

The Mentally-based being, on the other hand, often may speak to someone while doing other things and doesn't always check to see if the message has been received. A common scenario plays out with the Mentally-based person saying, "You don't understand what I am saying!" whereas the Emotional base will complain, "You don't get what I mean!" Remember, that was Harry and Frank's problem.

The Being: *(finally grasping the connection)* Thanks for explaining the difference to me. I noticed the friction between your pals Harry and Frank as you spoke of them with us at the Symposium, but I didn't fully grasp the extent of the problem.

Astro: *(wanting to be very clear)* I remind you it's not a question of better or worse. We all need and use both natures, along with the Physical, to integrate our base systems for fuller Self-expression. As I see it, we as individual Beings are like a beautiful, colored thread, who together weave a rich tapestry, more beautiful than any one thread by itself.

For compassion and understanding to connect, both the Mental and Emotional natures must be working together. In truth, we are all connected energetically and designed to work together while in these skin-suits.

And since this awareness sits in the Emotional body's jurisdiction, Understanding, which is the Mental's contribution, by itself lacks something to connect with. That's why Understanding is pointless without an experience to validate it.

The key is that only the Emotional body provides the *oomph!* to get us where we want to go. In truth—by virtue of our connected-ness with All That Is—it's where we already are, but don't know it!

To continue in this arena of connected-ness, the Emotional body is also the seat of our Heart energy, by connecting Heaven and Earth for us. What I mean by that, is that the entire universe is inside each of us, as us, or as our particular individual perception. Every one of us has an investment in feeling a part of something, that we are contributing to the larger picture. It isn't as though we need to do, be, or have every physical possibility, experience, or item that is available on planet Earth. Rather, like a good on-line catalog system in a library, it is comforting to know that we as individual terminals have access to the whole. The Emotional member's Heart energy or LOVE binds each of us as individuals to the whole.

The Being: *(enthused)* Wow! Do you mean to say that when I hear the phrase "LOVE is all that is," this is what it means?

Astro: *(speaking for itself)* I believe so. Most people have had at least one experience of this LOVE connection, but for those who haven't, it might seem impossible. It's not the kind of thing you can scientifically document, but you do know when you've felt it. For example, the LOVE connection demonstrates itself when a Mother soothes her child who has just fallen and scraped its knee . . . or when a friend shows a vote of confidence by giving you a thumbs up just before you go on stage to perform . . . or when you get a letter of acknowledgment from your boss for a job well done. And, of course, during a one-on-one relationship with another, love is the connection whereby you enjoy each other's presence simply by sitting quietly in each other's arms, watching a fire burn in the fireplace, or the encouragement to really discover that other person by giving them your full attention and listen-ability.

This brings up another strength of the Emotional nature's Heart/Love energy—the ability to risk, for one who loves, risks. The practical, security conscious, Mental nature cannot afford to risk being out of control, because there is equal possibility of loss as well as gain, and that is unacceptable to the Mental nature, when it is trying to protect the Being, or "do it right." Remember that protection, or imposed isolation, is truly not one of the Mental body's areas of jurisdiction, for that whole action of protection serves to move us out of participation.

Astro: *(really pleased with its own revelation)* Moving on, the Emotional nature not only houses the cleansers, but it also has the other healing factor given to us all, the gift of laughter. Laughter is not only a cleanser, but it is a means of lightening the load, freeing the Being or Spirit, and of not taking life quite so seriously. It heals the very core of our Essence— something you, the Being, are well aware of.

The Being: *(without hesitation)* It's true that as a Being of Light and Sound, it's important to me to feel buoyant, to see possibilities, and to laugh at myself. You cannot imagine, Astro, what things I can find to get all flustered over. Some items are really important, but many are not worth all of the energy I put into them.

Astro: *(identifying with the Being's comments)* Join the club. Remember, we all have an Ego body for a reason. If you don't stay actively interested in your own life's story, who else is going to? Or otherwise stated, only you are going to live your whole life with you—and no matter how dramatic your life experiences are, once heard, even repeatedly, they won't keep other people as interested in your life as you are. Everyone else is going to come and go, so it's up to you to motivate your Self in whatever endeavors that interest you or cross your path.

So, now, take a moment, Being, and let your Self filter this data, allowing your Emotional body to grow into its full potential expression. I remind you that your member could look the same as when it walked into the changing room, or it could appear in an entirely different form. We are simply allowing your natural creative imagination to do its job for you.

(after a pause) What do you see, Being?

The Being: *(looking intently)* Well, it's still the glowing, pulsating light, only I can feel that something is missing.

Astro: *(acknowledging the moment)* Okay, if that's the case, take a good look at your member, while I reiterate its jurisdictions. This body member houses the cleansers—the means for you, the Being, to clear out the internal closets of old hurts, resentments, and past experiences that keep you from fully being in the present moment.

It also "knows what it knows," which filters through your intuitive juices. This representative is the *connector* of Heart energy on all levels, between the Mental and Physical members, as well as the connector of you, the Being or Spirit, with all of totality—and you with other human Beings. The healing factor of laughter and the Heart/Love ability to risk are also in its realm. So, now, can you tell what is missing?

(the Being envisions the many attributes over and over, and finally realizes what was not fully present, as a gleam comes into Its energy field . . .)

The Being: *(full of lightness)* I've got it! I was so thrilled to see the sparkle that I didn't notice that the LOVE connection wasn't as full as I know it to be for me. It's as though this member looked more like my Mental one. And, as glad as I am to find the Amethyst Crystal, I don't view the Heart energy in the same way. I now know what my Emotional body member looks like!

(And before their very eyes, both Astro and the Being watch as the bright, glowing light changes into the Being's one-time adult pet dog, whose name had been Gabriella. The Being is

*filled with tears of joy and wonderment to see Gabriella
again, for her beloved companion had passed away five years
previously.)*

*(Then, true to her nature, and as if to let the Being know that
she is overjoyed to be able to reach the Being again, and that
she is truly with the Being always, Gabriella bounds over to
the Being and begins enthusiastically to lick Its hint of a face,
and the Being knows Itself as complete, unconditional LOVE,
Loving, and Loved.)*

*(Just then, the Being finds Its Self hugging tightly all three of
Its members, plus Astro, until they unintentionally nearly
choke the life force out of the Body Therapist.)*

Astro: *(croaking)* Whoa! I need some air.

The Being, with Amethyst Crystal, Unicorn, and Gabriella chiming in:
So sorry.

*(to say the body members are glad to be re-united is an
understatement . . .)*

Astro: *(sighing with relief at completing these processes)* I'm glad
you are all in support of each other. Bear in mind that you can
call a meeting of your board members anytime, anywhere.
You can meet out in the cosmos, on a mountaintop, on the
toilet, or whenever the need arises to handle a situation, to
processing an experience or point of view, or just for FUN.
Any one of the members or you, yourself, Being, may call the
meeting. You can also use board meetings to handle items
from the past by either re-arranging the data to complete the
situation, or by reformulating the data or scenario to suit your
evolving personal standards.

And, with the Board Room process being complete, and with all three members fully present, now you are ready to hear—having reached a point of listen-ability—about what I call the nature of Typical Reality, and the more practical side of this transformational practice.

*. . . Love
is in our hearts
and can be expressed
through our heads . . .
. . . our 'fears'
develop in our heads,
and prevent us from being close
to our hearts.*

—Brock Tully, *Reflections for Someone Special*

Resentment is the flip side of appreciation.
—Tom White

Where you tend a rose, a thistle cannot grow.
—Frances Hodgson Burnett, *The Secret Garden*

♡ CHAPTER EIGHT ♡

THE NATURE OF TYPICAL REALITY

(The Being, Amethyst Crystal, Unicorn, and Gabriella together make a joint effort to quiet their joyful reunion and to give their full attention back to receiving Astro's next instruction.)

Astro: *(acknowledging their happiness in a knowing manner)* **Now** that your members are fully present and in support of you and each other, I'd like to take a moment and share with you a fable to illustrate a point, that of "How People Usually Operate in Life From the Standpoint of Each of Their Members," and I believe you will find it to be quite a typical human scenario. To make it easier to understand, Being, I will speak in the first person, as though the plot were my situation, and I will arbitrarily choose the female gender from which to narrate this tale. So, once again I invite you and all your members to make yourselves comfortable, stretch out in the grass, close your eyes, and enjoy the warmth of the sun's rays as I begin . . . .

It all starts on a Thursday night, with my husband asking me, "What are you doing tomorrow night?"

Without really answering, I reply, "Why do you ask?"

He says, "Because I'd like to ask you out for a date." (We like to continue our romance as much as possible.)

"Owwww," I groan, "I have to work tomorrow night." Case closed. With a forlorn look of sadness, I cuddle up next to him and ask, "I sure hope you'll ask me again?"

And he replies, "Sure, next month, like clockwork."

Well, then I start figuring. Next month being eleven whole days away, and I really begin to feel as though I'm about to miss out on something by not going out with my husband tomorrow night. But what can I do about it?

Perhaps I can say that I am sick and can't make the appointment, or I could just cancel due to personal reasons—but either way I would be undermining my own standards and integrity, which I have noticed tends to work like a boomerang and come back to haunt me. After all, if I don't keep my word, how can I expect others to keep theirs? However, not wanting to miss out on a wonderful evening, my members and I begin to plot out a plan of action to solve this dilemma.

So then, away we go at it, my Mental, Physical, and Emotional members, and I.

At our earliest convenience, which happens to be during the night—my Board Members call a meeting in one of their favorite forest settings to discuss the matter at hand. The Physical body representative opens up with, "I know! I'll say she (the Being) is tired. After all, she *did* get up early yesterday morning, and today, well, it was earlier than usual—which isn't very early—and tomorrow morning she's set to get up ahead of schedule. So, I'll let her know that the day simply looks too long and that *something* has got to go."

At this notion, the Mental body representative chimes in with, "What about the possibility that she simply postpone the session to a later date?"

This brings a moan from the Emotional body representative, who complains, "But there *is* no other time that isn't already overloaded! I just can't deal with one more change in schedule. You, our Mental genius, forget that I have to provide the *oomph!* to get the Physical to execute these great ideas of yours. Quite frankly, I get pooped out."

"Okay, okay," concedes the Mental member, "but, how do we get out of doing the work and still enjoy the evening without feeling guilty or without being stressed out from having to rearrange things? Also, we want to make sure you, our Emotional member, can provide her with enough energy to be enthused and go on the date in the first place."

"Not to worry" offers the Physical member brightly, "— I'll just see to it that she is only mildly wasted, so she doesn't feel she has the strength to work but is well enough to enjoy the date."

"Sounds good to me," pipe in both the Mental and Emotional Board Members.

And so, the stage is set. . . .

Upon awakening, even after having slept almost eight full hours, I (the Being) notice my body feels as though it has been mowed down by a Mack truck.

The Mind then kicks in with, "Boy, do I feel tired—and I have such a hectic day planned. I sure wish I wasn't working tonight."

As a Being, I then react to this with complete Mental override: "Oh well, just do it, and don't agonize that you set all of this in motion!"—not realizing that my members are purposely trying to get me out of working and on to the date this evening.

Then the Mind plays its next card, as I hear within, "You know you don't have to visit your Aunt again this week—"

—to which I have to counter, out loud, "But being gone for the next *four* weeks, I just feel like I need to." So, now then, off I go . . .

Of course, by now I (the Being) am running a full half-hour behind my plans, even though I had plenty of time to be ready sooner. So, as I set out, anxiousness sets in, as I try to drive the ninety-odd miles as quickly as possible to reach the senior housing where my Aunt lives.

About now the Emotional body puts in its contribution via the Physical form: "I'm really feeling the tiredness in my body, and I'm wondering seriously if I'll ever get a vacation from life"—while I (the Being) still don't grasp why I'm becoming more and more agitated with the day.

By the time I reach my destination, I am almost angry with myself, as I have only a few hours to be with my aunt, having frittered away a portion of it just not getting going.

To seal the upset, the Mental nature offers up, philosophically, "Oh well, there's nothing I can do about it now," which does nothing to lift my spirits.

However, by now I am completely off base Emotionally, and testy with my eighty-six-year-old Aunt, while my Mental nature grows increasingly impatient to find a few moments to itself, because the issue of what to do this evening has not been handled and is therefore overrunning the moment. This all results in an okay visit, but not as fun and free as usual.

So, back on the road three hours later, I am beginning to feel Physically ill.

Not surprisingly, the Physical body announces, "I simply can't work tonight; I'm too ill."

At this, the Emotional body finds itself in a complete quandary. "So, if you are too tired and ill to work," it cries, "just how do you plan to have enough energy to go out on a date with your husband?"—already feeling the impact of not staying true to my own values.

"Well," the Mental body balks, "that really does put us members in a pickle. Besides, we still haven't uncovered a date to change the appointment to!"

By now, the Physical body is screaming the loudest, as this is the one who has had to hold all this ongoing conflict all day, "Take me home! I don't want to do errands or go swimming for exercise. All I want to do is to get between the sheets and stay there!" And with that outburst, it stomps out of the forest they were lounging in.

"So now what do we do?" wails the Emotional body member. "We have gotten ourselves into a no-win situation—and all we wanted was to go out tonight and have a little fun!"

With the one Board Member out of the clearing, the meeting has for the moment ground to a halt, leaving the Mental and Emotional bodies at an impasse, for without the form to function in, thoughts and feelings are merely vibrating energy, without direction. Operating in a semi-automatic state, without the benefit of the presence of all members, I do manage to run the necessary errands, after which the Mental body suddenly wakes up and issues an idea-memo over the intercom to the Physical body's office: "So, just go to the club and let yourself enjoy the water—but don't make yourself have to swim the forty laps!"

The Physical body, after considering the thought, begrudgingly agrees, "Okay."

At this, the Emotional body holds its tongue, anticipating the outcome, for it knows that exercise is one of the best ways to release energy that is pent up from either frustration or elation, and the Physical body *might* just have the chance to experience for itself its rejuvenation, which might then enable it to re-enter the forest and the conversation, so that a real joint solution will have a chance of emerging.

And, lo and behold, the steam room and jacuzzi feels great, and so does the forty laps, as well as a few minutes in the dry sauna—and—guess what!—the Physical body is now doing great, again ready to participate in the remaining events of the day, just as reality hits its awareness.

"Oh no!" objects the Physical system.

"Oh, yes!" shouts the Emotional system triumphantly. "Now you feel well enough to work!"

Jumping into the debate, the Mental body quickly puts in with, "Yes, but how about offering the client a Monday night appointment, which just opened up? Then we can feel great, go out on the date, and still get the work done!"

"Now wait just a minute!" cautions the Emotional member. "This client is anticipating the work tonight. Do you think it's fair to jack her around—just because you want to squeeze in one more experience for tonight? I can hardly believe you even suggested it!"

"Now we're back at the beginning," complains the Mind, "and time is running short. Well, I guess we'll just have to go through with it. The car is half-packed by now and our clothes are changed, so, let's just go ahead with it. . . . ."

In the car, still wanting to shift things somehow, and completely frustrated by the course things have taken, the tears began to roll down my (the Being's) face.

"If only Ella were here!" sobs the Emotional member. (Ella was my childhood dog—the one who always listened to my woes.) "Then I'd feel more like going. Especially with her as copilot."

This release by the Emotional body helps all three bodies relax a little, as is usually the case, and eventually a spurt of natural enthusiasm surfaces, enough so that, by the time my members and I arrive at our destination, all the conflict and anguish are gone, and the session with my client ends up going beautifully. . . .

(the Being sits in thoughtful silence, absorbing the import of Astro's story)

Astro: *(after a few moments)* Did you notice anything in particular about this story as a whole?

The Being: *(slightly uncertain of Astro's meaning)* I'm not sure what you are asking for, but it seems to me that it had a lot of *effort* in it. There was a lot of going around and around, without any change in the eventual outcome.

Astro: *(smiling)* Exactly. It takes a great deal of energy to counter yourself, or to attempt to go against your own standards or integrity. So, take a good look and see what *you* might do differently in the same situation—now that your members are fully available to you for self-expression.

The Being: Well . . . *(pausing to gather Its thoughts)* first of all, if it were me, my Mental member would support me from the start by reminding me and the other bodies that when words and action match, what results is commitment, the most powerful statement I can make as a human Being. So, keeping the appointment, short of physical illness, would be a given. And, Emotionally speaking, since the Emotional member experiences everything in the present moment, I could realize that looking forward to my date is actually just as much fun as the event itself, so planning for another day would be easy. On the Physical level, being present is the best opportunity to have a full experience, so I would be reminded to be present with my Aunt, my swimming, and my work, enabling me to end the day with even more energy than when I started.

Astro: *(really proud of the Being's grasp of Its members' strengths)* How marvelous! Do you notice how everyone wins in such a revised scenario?

The Being: *(somewhat surprised)* Why, yes, and I wasn't even viewing the situation with that notion in mind. How does that work, exactly?

Astro: *(immediately responding)* Good question—and to answer it I'd like to share with you exactly how the members interact. For example, when you are standing on a curb getting ready to cross the street, what do you do first, automatically, before you cross?

(The Being looks puzzled, not quite sure what Astro is looking for . . . .)

Astro: *(mildly teasing)* Don't work so hard! These are not trick questions.

The Being: *(somewhat hesitantly)* Well, all I can think of is, look both ways and check for traffic?

Astro: *(pressing ahead firmly)* Very good. And if you saw a car coming from the right, what does your Mental nature do automatically in reference to that vehicle?

The Being: *(still wondering why this line of questioning)* I guess it would figure out about how fast the car is coming, to see if I have time to cross.

Astro: *(exultantly)* Bingo! So anytime you are looking for information that concerns the past or future, whether distant or immediate, the Mental member is going to be involved. Got it?

The Being: *(the internal lights come on)* Aha! You're saying that I'll always know when the Mental body is to be consulted—because some element of past or future is being addressed.

Astro: *(emphatically)* Right! Now remember, the Mental nature deals only with data and information and with supporting the distribution of that data or information. Whenever it *judges*, *criticizes*, *negates*, or *limits*, it is undermining the work either of the Emotional or the Physical body member, each of whom operate fully in the moment and handle, very capably, all momentary concerns.

In addition, suppose I said to you that we were going to take a hike, and, by the way, it will be for one hundred miles.

Gabriella: *(rolling its eyes)* Yeah . . . right!

Amethyst Crystal: *(jokingly)* Sure thing.

Astro: *(attempting to look sternly at the Mental and Emotional body members but not quite succeeding)* I don't recall asking for commentary.

Gabriella and Amethyst Crystal: *(chuckling to themselves)* Okay, okay, we just couldn't pass it up. Please do go on.

Astro: *(still trying to keep a straight face)* As I was saying, for a hundred-mile hike, which body member is going to be in charge of putting one foot in front of the other?

The Being: *(beaming)* That's easy—the Physical body representative. . . . my beautiful Unicorn! *(The Being strokes its velvety smooth, soft, white mane . . . .)*

Astro: *(with a mischievous gleam in its energy field)* Now you may have to ponder this next one. Say you are in an Art Gallery, standing in front of a particular painting, and I come along and ask you, "What do you think about this painting?"

What do you have to do first, before you can answer the question?

(the Being envisions Itself in front of a painting and attempts to locate the answer to Astro's question, but nothing comes up)

The Being: *(trying hard but unsuccessfully to think of an answer)* I'm sorry, but I just can't figure out what you are looking for.

Astro: *(knowingly)* No problem, Being. This question appears to be an easy one, but it's really not. The answer I am looking for is not in the Mental or the Physical body's jurisdiction, for it deals with *presence*. Before you can tell anyone about the painting, you must first *be* with it. What I mean is be *present*, feel it, "get" it—which in this case does not include either Physical movement *or* Mental input.

The Being: *(catching the meaning)* Oh, I get it. I have to use my senses, so to speak—either touch it, see it, taste it, or hear it, or otherwise have a *feeling* about it, right? And then, the Physical gathers in these perceptions and makes them available to the Mental member to analyze and respond.

Astro: *(confirming the Being's understanding)* That's right. Because the Physical and Emotional bodies do not have to interpret each other's domain, they can get direct information from the other in any given moment. This is why they are so often linked together as one unit, even though their areas of concern and expertise are very different. It's only when the *experience* has reached the Physical form and registered as a *feeling* of some kind that the Mental nature can take the data and figure out what's to take place next.

The Being: *(pausing to ponder the implications)* So now I know *how* each member enters a given scenario, but what about accessing them when they are blocked or just not functioning fully?

Astro: *(considering the best way to respond)* To answer your question, I need to tell you how each of the three natures holds its information.

The Physical form holds the data and experiences of the other team players until it is full up and overflowing, at which time it will shut down for repairs. Short of that point, however, this densest body, having no tendency to pass any kind of judgment, simply "sits" in the data until we (the Being) direct the removal through the Mental body, Emotional body, or a combination of these two members—with thoughts eventually being released through the wrists and ankles, and emotions through the pores of the skin.

In the Physical form, an Emotionally-based being can literally *sit* in its emotions, because its nature is located from the lower back down into the buttocks area and legs. These folks tend to carry more weight in the hips and thighs. And, in the middle of an upset, they literally withdraw from participating by withholding their thoughts and feelings, thereby taking the whole situation personally and seriously. One very powerful way to lighten this stuck-ness is by vocalizing. Either sing in the car along with one of your favorite artists, howl at the moon like a wolf, practice "toning," or shout at the top of your lungs (preferably not *at* another Being). This vocalizing action moves the energy that has been blocked at the waist and which sits deep in the solar plexus. It allows the Being to go way down deep inside itself and release the thick, heavy stuff that it is currently experiencing or holding.

I've noticed that when a person is Emotionally stuck, they aren't usually real excited to say or do much of anything. In fact, the degree to which a person is not conversive can tell you just how upset they really are. For example, if you ask them a question and get only yes, no, or one-word answers, then they are quite probably angry but not fully shut down, but if you try to converse with someone who appears to have nothing at all to say, you can bet they are *livid* inside.

After some enthusiastic vocalizing in whatever way works for the Being—or by having someone just "hear" their concerns without "doing" anything about the information, such as giving advice or passing judgments—quite often that great emotional healer, laughter, surfaces, which uplifts the Spirit, the Being, the Essence, the Self, or whatever you wish to call the energy field that is you.

Once the Emotional system gets in motion again, items of concern can be resolved, a re-alignment with the whole can be experienced, and a re-newed vitality for living can emerge. All-in-all, a person feels better and has a better out-look on life and on others who are in one's life, even if the circumstances haven't changed a bit.

The Mental strength or Mentally-based Being, on the other hand, spends a great deal of time in the body's penthouse (i.e., the brain), and so its focal point is from the lower back up the body into the head, neck, and shoulder areas. When the Mental nature thinks no one cares anyway, so why bother, it will tend to stay stuck in generalities, blame, shame, guilt, and absolutely no forgiveness. "No give," so to speak. To release this patterning, such a person can take a moment alone, close their eyes, and envision the person or situation that appears to be activating the upset. In this vision, using the natural, creative talents of the mind, it can say exactly what it's thinking in any terms it wants, for this is a safe arena to do so without placing the thoughts full of garbage (judgment, etc.) on anyone else.

To summarize the distinctions between the way the two natures hold their information, let me give you some of their attributes more succinctly, before continuing. For example, in upset, the Emotional nature MUST withdraw—they must appear "shut down" to others, in order to resolve the increasing Emotional imbalance within themselves, which the situation has been activating. The Mental nature, on the other hand, will appear to go on the attack to resolve the misinterpretation of its perception of the situation, in an attempt to reach understanding. Even though the Emotional system resolves things in the moment, if the input becomes too much from its vantage point, a type of paralysis sets in. On the other hand, even though the Mental system prefers to move the item OUT of the moment to be handled, it will "push and push and push the point"—wanting to understand it NOW—if the upset is too great.

And, before you ask, the Emotionally-based Being with a Mental override can *really* find itself caught between suppressed feelings and denied concerns—giving itself the conflicting signals of "WITHDRAW!" and "ATTACK!" simultaneously, because both its Mental and Emotional natures are desiring balance in each of their domains at the same time. The bottom line is, for the Mental body's blockages—which often result in headaches, shoulder pain, and restricted neck movement—to be removed, the Mental nature needs to *hear* itself. It can do this through "visionization" or in talking with another person. It's slightly harder with another person, because that person may react, whereas in the vision, the people or situation can only "get" by nodding their heads or be on the receiving end of the communication.

At the very least, our Mental activity wants to be allowed to figure things out. That's right, it wants and needs to tell its story, and usually with all of the details, taking the time to filter all of the factors involved and to figure out what value the data has for it. Because people from the Mental standpoint pride themselves on getting things just right, it's important to most Mental natures to remember specific names, dates, and places as they share their stories, which usually drives the Emotionally-based natures nuts! *(chuckling)* For, once the Emotional nature gets the drift of the conversation, all added information is extraneous to it, so it stops listening or attempts to begin speaking over the other person.

Another way the Mental body or Mentally-based Being continues its protection patternings is through remembering and rehashing the upset verbally with as many people as possible who will listen to their woes.

The Being: *(internally recognizing instances when It has experienced the traits described by Astro, both within Its Self and with others)*

I'm beginning to "get" how the members hold or express an upset.

Astro: *(bringing the point full circle)* Yes, and what goes on within us when we are not understood, grasped, or Self-loved is a buildup of bitterness and resentment, and before long, we are at-a-tilt, literally fighting gravity to stay upright, and fighting our Selves to remain present. The result can be physical dis-"ease."

Taken to an extreme, you have the case of the Walking Dead—a person who appears to function, but has no spark of life. This condition is also known as "total overwhelm," "being shut down," or having "no one at home." Many of these terms relate to not wanting to be here in form on the planet to one degree or another.

Amethyst Crystal: *(really wanting to understand this idea)* Just a moment, Astro. Can you be a little more specific about what you mean by "at-a-tilt"?

Astro: *(happy to oblige)* Certainly, Amethyst. In fact, this concept affects each of you members, which many times results in the Being's discomfort in Self-expressing. It's a little like the three-legged stool. When one leg is extra long (over-developed), the stool is at-a-tilt. Or when one leg is shorter or missing altogether, again the stool tilts, and balance is no longer possible. I believe I mentioned earlier the example of a child who is exceptionally bright and put ahead in school, leaving the Emotional and Physical members at risk of having less natural support in their growth. That is one way in which at-a-tilt-ness can be expressed.

Also, within the Physical form itself also exist three facets that promote movement and our ability to grow and change. Those more concrete aspects are the skeletal, muscular, and nervous systems. Even though they are only three of the many systems our Physical forms maintain, they must work together to keep us physically upright and not at odds with gravity. Furthermore, adding insult to injury, if the Physical body is at-a-tilt within itself, with nerves, muscles, and bones out of alignment, it's even harder for the Being to stay balanced and handle stress. Then, with gravity relentlessly pulling down on us all the time, our resolves tend to weaken along with our ability to deal with life. Again, the key to Physical balance lies with *integrating* all the three skeletal, muscular, and nervous systems for fluid, effortless motion and inner and outer strength, along with the Mental and Emotional team players.

As another example, if you hold a grudge toward someone, the fuel of your Mental nature, as it reminds yourself to continue to view that person from that begrudging vantage point, pulls you out of the moment you are having—completely negating any current Physical and Emotional inputs. Otherwise stated, it's like living in the past, disregarding the present, and ignoring the future. A similar imbalance occurs during infatuation or extreme fascination, such as when the Being meets someone and all seems fine for a couple of weeks or months, then bam! the other person disappears, stops calling—or begins to appear less wonderful in daily concerns. The Mental body desperately looks for the lesson from this past event, and at the same time looks for, hopes for, and "obsesses" about possible future encounters or opportunities to resolve or understand the situation, again completely pulling the Being out of availability for the present moment. This is attachment, and the Mental will never know for sure what happened, for there is no certainty in the Mental nature; knowing-ness is in the Emotional's realm. As the Mental member takes over the moment, it obliterates any enjoyment possibilities that might otherwise be available from what is happening in the Eternal Moment of Now. This at-a-tilt-ness can be a very PAINful condition, as the members become excruciatingly estranged from their natural functioning.

Another example might be living with someone or putting up with a situation you really dislike, yet feeling trapped and unable to leave the relationship. Now the Emotional nature will keep you in constant turmoil over your predicament, which looks hopeless to you. Your value is depleted, and you find yourself numb most of the time or plotting ways in your mind to get away from this person or situation. Again, you are focused in one arena only (even though the Physical is overly impacted with Emotional upset), and life in general looks to be a major burden and a royal pain in the neck. In such a state, reaction rather than creation becomes the *modus operandi*.

In any event, all such misalignments, either Mentally or Emotionally held, may eventually drop the Physical body's ability to regenerate itself, down to below the fifty percent mark, at which point we as human Beings move into survival tactics. In other words, whenever a Being's ability to be fully present falls below the fifty percent point, they *must* obtain the rest of their energy from another person; they aren't holding enough vital energy to regenerate their own life force, and we see these people as "desperate," "needy," "nervous," and so on.

This use of others' energy takes many forms, some subtle and some not so subtle. As one common example, have you noticed that when experiencing ill-ness, people often look to others to "validate" them in their "invalid" state? Unfortunately, this puts their three dense bodies even further at odds with their individual areas of jurisdiction and therefore at odds with the Being who lives in that body, and thus also at odds with the universe at large, which, mirror-like, simply reflects all of these incongruencies.

Unfortunately, most of us, adults as well as children, are taught—largely by unconscious agreement—that there is only a limited amount of energy for such regeneration available to us, and furthermore that we are all after the same limited supply. So, when we are not heard or "gotten" as we would like to be—and we slip below that fifty percent mark in our at-a-tilt-ness, we end up vying for attention as a basic means of survival in our roles as siblings, parents, and adults. This striving to get re-filled through others is a real hit-or-miss proposition, and it can result in a feeling of being drained, because we don't have any guarantee that the others will always be available to us when we need them to be.

Besides that, most of us have not been trained to re-fill the Spirit through universal means.

The Being: *(with active curiosity)* Hold on, Astro! Just what exactly do you mean by "universal" means?

Astro: *(again glad to know the Being is paying attention)* What I'm referring to, Being, is a feeling of connected-ness with all of the vibration and energy that makes up our reality, of being able to replenish the Self by accessing the greater Self, known as "all of totality" or "one-ness." It's rather hard to describe that which is greater than definition, and that which can only be experienced as true. I can only say that for anyone who has had this feeling occur within themselves, it makes perfect sense.

The ability to experience *balance* within our totality lies in our ability to grasp the fullness of our nature, i.e., both the Mental and the Emotional input in relation to the Physical, in this Eternal Moment of Now. I'd best describe this like an airplane. The Eternal Moment of Now is the body of the plane; the left wing represents the past, and the right wing, the future. If we dwell on the past, cast blame, or refuse to forgive and forget as we are learning our lessons—as in the saying, "The future will be just like the past"—the wing dips to the left, flying the whole plane at a tilt, as upset and fear become prevalent.

The same holds true for the future. The person who says, "The past is gone—just forget it; today is brand new, and what came before it doesn't matter," negates the lessons we have learned in the past, which affect the lessons we are in the process of learning now. By judging and categorizing our past experiences as irrelevant, the right wing now leans heavily toward the ground. Either extreme produces only an illusion of complete control, and both hinder the integration of the lesson at hand.

The order of events in how we learn our lessons goes something like this:

One: When I don't know I'm flaky, I have flaky friends.
Two: When I am conscious of flaky-ness, I will get angry when someone is flaky around me, and point out the flaky-ness of others, with or without perceiving my own flaky-ness.
Three: When I deal with my own flaky-ness and move out of the consciousness of flaky-ness, I will no longer have flaky friends.

You see, we learn our lessons through interactions with others, and we can know when a lesson is complete for ourselves when it no longer surfaces in our conversation.

However, only when we feel safety, do we give ourselves the go ahead light to have an experience when we're having it. When we're criticized and lose that feeling of safety, we shut down the lesson and revert to past/future survival, blanking out our center of balance, which is designed to neutralize the illusion of isolation and separation that brings on attacks and defense mechanisms.

As a Being successfully moves its members towards integration, and the Mental and Emotional bodies release and re-align, the Physical form also goes through metamorphosis. Often during this shifting, further Physical aches and pains occur, as it takes four to six weeks for changes on the Mental level to open the door to integrate into the Physical and

Emotional systems as a new habit energy. Since we appear to function in habitual form—why not have it be habits we like and do effortlessly.

However, once any bit of information, lesson, or item that was previously held as unconscious habit energy gets to the conscious level, your life is really on the line!

The Being: *(startled and alarmed)* Good gracious! *(seeing that Astro is not laughing)* You can't be serious about that; I mean, I thought we had just saved our life, and now you're saying this whole process puts us further at risk!

(the Being throws Its arms protectively around Gabriella, Amethyst Crystal, and Unicorn)

Astro: *(sincerely)* Well, you have saved your life in the sense that you have come into a powerful alignment and have some new-found abilities to operate in an INTEGRATED capacity of wholeness. However, before this took place, your ignorance was a kind of innocent bliss, because unconscious energy does not attract its opposite as vibrantly as conscious energy does. As your particular lessons and tendencies become conscious energy, it will tend to attract its opposite. Or, in the words of Peace Pilgrim, "If we are out of harmony through ignorance, we suffer somewhat; but if we *know better* and are still out of harmony, then we suffer a great deal."

For example, when someone living and talking from habitual fear becomes *conscious* of sending that vibration out, and when someone else who is at-a-tilt picks it up, WHAM-O!— you have impact. The newly conscious energy attracts its opposite like a lightning rod. Many people recognize such episodes as "tests." Eventually the charge dissipates as the

Being learns to stay conscious, balanced, and in alignment while the new habit energy replaces the at-a-tilt-ness, as in the "flaky-ness" example, where eventually the opposite energy disappears along with the languaging related to the lesson.

We also want to remember that since we all have different temperaments and lessons, this results in different responses to similar stimuli. One person's feeling of abandonment because they couldn't go to the store with their Mom, is another child's opportunity to be home alone in peace and harmony. It is up to each of us to realize at what pace we grow, *knowing* that every experience or circumstance is only an opportunity. Some we take, some we don't.

On another level, the wings of the plane we were discussing can be equated to the Emotional and Mental bodies. The left wing equals the Emotional, the right wing equals the Mental, with the body of the plane being the Physical body. If one Emotionally "flies off the handle" or erupts into upset every time there is a change in life, the Physical form is put through tremendous energy changes and requires more *oomph!* to appear "all together." Plus, if you've ever been around someone who is totally out of control or balance, you literally don't know where you stand with that person and so are unable to relax as well. The same can be said for the Mental nature. While in full control, it negates the worth of the Emotional body's input and withholds the sharing of the Self, flying rigidly on sheer logic, reason, and rationale. It becomes obvious that we can use the Mental power either to support ourselves or to destroy ourselves.

A Being who is at-a-tilt must get all three foundation systems up to speed and into alignment in order to integrate, balance, and align with its true personal worth. The truth just IS, and we can make it look any way we like through our Mental capacities—but if it is not tempered with the knowing-ness of the Emotional nature, we are once again flying at a tilt, and we experience fear and uncertainty regarding our personal value. For the Mental nature doesn't have a clue as to our value—its natural gift is in support of the Self—no matter if we do life right, wrong, upside down, backwards, inside out, or topsy-turvy. Otherwise stated, when your words and actions match, with your Mental and Emotional members working together for the totality of you, the results are evident in the Physical form, and you exude well-"Being"-ness: the plane flies smoothly.

You may have heard the phrase, "Where you tend a rose, a thistle cannot grow." This means that when the head is full of constructive thoughts and the heart full of happiness, there is no room for negative judgments, criticisms, limitations, fears, angers, resentments, and so on. I know I don't need to remind you of the opposite, that when the head is full of nasty thoughts, there is no room for good ones. Rest assured that who you "see" is what you get, and that you are the one who determines the place from which you view all of reality: if you see caring, then you get caring. If you see manipulation, you get manipulation. If you see through the filter of prejudice, then you get prejudice, and so on.

It's been my observation in my "mini-surveys," that when the Being moves into the state of balance, it is much less likely to overlay its point of view onto another Being, and a feeling of safety to Self-express emerges, both for that Being and an-other, resulting in a feeling of connected-ness. Or, otherwise stated, to the degree we are focused on our own evolution, we are less likely to bother others in their chosen form of growth and Self-expression.

(Astro pauses briefly, musing to itself)

(again sharing its thoughts out loud) Interestingly enough, it is the freedom of creative thought that allows for this experience of wholeness. And yet, it is often the Mental nature which tries to limit that very freedom by describing the situation rather than just "Be" in it. *(chuckling)* It's no wonder the Mental and Emotional members can get at such odds with each other.

Likewise, when it comes to communications between people—the members of the larger Self or totality—when conversing with an Emotionally-based Being, in order to achieve clarity, you must constantly ask, "What did you mean by what you said?"—because the Mental nature will very likely figure out some other meaning for the very same words. And when dealing with a Mentally-based Being, it is imperative to bring them into the moment as much as possible by asking, "What are you feeling in your body right now?" As they stop to look, they often discover triggered emotions that were in the process of being buried because they were embarrassing, were deemed unimportant, or might make the Being too vulnerable and unprotected.

Have you heard, Being, the word "assumed," broken down?

The Being: *(almost startled by the question)* No, not really. I don't quite know what you mean.

Astro: *(knowingly)* Well, if you separate the letters into three parts like this: ASS-U-ME—you can see that it carries a new meaning. When we assume something, we put clarity at risk.

If we don't ask enough questions to clear up the confusion in our own minds, or think we heard what another said but don't bother to check, we literally make an ass of both you and me, by filling in the blanks ourselves, which may or may not match the other person's thoughts, and thus the feelings of separation get strengthened. As marvelous as habit energy can be when it is habits we like, it can be murderous with items about our Self that we are not as fond of.

The Being: *(excited, with interest piqued)* Whoa, Astro. What exactly is this Habit Energy business, anyway?

Astro: *(very amused)* There I go again—like that fish in water story you shared—what is obvious to me I sometimes forget to cover completely as I speak. I should probably clarify that when I refer to "habit energy," I'm referring to the unconscious behavior patterns that are harmful or that we don't care for—as opposed to the supportive ones. These negative habit energies originate during a survival mode, when a person learns to suppress their emotions as a matter of basic survival (often by age seven to ten, by which time most of our belief systems have become set). This negative habit energy is stored deeply in the Mental nature. That's why you can meet someone, and everything seems okay, because their habit energy will declare everything is "okay, fine," when in reality they are sitting on a volcano of emotions. Then out of what seems like a clear blue sky, all craziness breaks loose, the emotions run high, and they seem like a completely different person. Actually, the habit energy tends to go on line directly on top of such a person's control buttons. Then when either their safety becomes threatened or a crisis occurs, their Emotional truth emerges with all of its compressed fury. It usually takes a crisis to remove the clamps that have been holding the negative habit energy on line.

Just clearing up this one point—of not assuming things in our relationships and dealing with unconscious thoughts, feelings, and actions—has temendous potential for expanding our awareness, both of ourselves and the world around us.

The key to living life is to let your Self fully have "where you are at"—whatever that may be. Only through fully experiencing "where you are at" at the moment allows you to get on to the next item that comes up for you—by not resisting the moment of awareness, by being able to sit in embarrassment or any non-agreement, and by backing yourself one hundred percent, even when you fall "short of the mark." Being "exactly where you are at" completes the moment for you and gives you the "space" to create a new position to sit in, in the next Eternal Moment of Now.

(the group falls into a silent reverie)

So—Being, Gabriella, Unicorn, and Amethyst Crystal—do you have any other questions you'd like to have answered before we return to the Symposium?

(Unicorn, the beautiful, white, glowing, Physical body representative, who has been sitting patiently while the Being, Gabriella, and Amethyst Crystal sort out so many confusing notions, has one thought persistently remaining—and, breaking the momentary silence, it poses its question to Astro for the group. . . .)

Unicorn: *(in a very soft but penetrating voice)* So tell us, Astro, just exactly what is "true reality"?

Fish in water,
bird in air,
humanity in life.

—Chinese proverb

Life in harmony with creation
knows what is real—true reality.
God, or all-of-totality,
connects through the Heart
and is supported through Mind.

The real truth for you is going to come
from true self-acceptance and no place else.

—from *The Right Use of Will*

. . . in 'wanting'
i give to receive,
in 'loving'
i receive from giving.

—Brock Tully, *Reflections for Someone Special*

228

Birth as a human being is considered a rare gift.

—Sri Sathya Sai Baba

♡ CHAPTER NINE ♡

TRUE REALITY

Astro: *(sighing to itself)* You know, it is much easier to explain typical reality, because there are so many examples of it currently on planet Earth. Then, what we generally call "reality" is but a preconceived agreement, whereas actually life is not as defined as we have been led to believe, such as having been told all our lives that we had to color only within the lines! Rather, there are lots of experiences beyond today's agreed-upon reality that are REAL, and we are the receivers of this vast, endless energy of wonder. For example, in 1900, the idea of turning on an electronic device such as a television and seeing what's going on in Australia would have been discounted as "unreal," but today it is most accepted. Another very familiar reality change came with the advent of the airplane. After all, barf bags were placed on airplanes for a reason, because flying in the air truly did not match people's belief systems, and their stomachs responded. Today, although barf bags are still available, they're rarely used.

True reality is also challenging to describe, because we are limited to what I call "form" terms, which are words to describe what appears to be in form or visible, whereas what we are really looking for is a way to explain *energy*. It's as though the English language is inadequate to describe that which appears abstractual but in true reality is quite real and tangible!

I suppose you all noticed that I use some words that may not be in your dictionary, and yet their meanings are "get"-able. For example, I often use the words *misnomer, misperception, visionize, disparancy, wonderment, notion, "be"-fundled, lip-flappers* (human Beings), *mis-cue, at-a-tilt, abstractual,* and many words from the *Ness* family: *Being-ness, connected-ness, knowing-ness, one-ness, well-ness,* and so on.

The key or underlying similarity of energy for all these terms is that they don't carry "riders." I consider a rider to be any word that carries, beyond its meaning, some form of negative judgment. After all, we like *assertive* people, but generally speaking we can do without the really *aggressive* ones. *Assertive* has positive connotations, while *aggressive* implies running over another's thoughts, feelings, and/or actions— thereby running over that person's value as a Priceless Gift.

(Astro pauses a moment in reflection . . .)

I mean, doesn't it strike you funny that there are very few new words in the English language, except from the technological fields (i.e., science, medicine, computers). *(half muttering to itself)* It certainly piques my curiosity, I'll tell you.

(regaining its focus) In any event, to address true reality, I believe it would be helpful if I expanded on the levels of awareness in which we are known to function in daily life. For purposes of aligning our greater "Self" with this notion of individual selves in separate bodies, I have focused on the

three densest systems—Physical, Mental, and Emotional—
for they are always in operation in third-dimensional experiences. I have referred to these systems as Bodies in their own
right to give them definition, a means for human understanding, and a way to see exactly how human "Beings" are
received out in the world at large.

In truth, these members of your Self-expressive team—
physical form, creative thoughts, and momentary feelings—
are not only designed to integrate, but inter-relate as well, and
occasionally merge to create a magical moment. Therefore, it
is most important to feel *one* with your members, talk with
your members, and appreciate the intricacies that go into the
action of full "Being"-ness or "Self"-expression in your
home, on the job, and with family and friends.

Another way to "hold" these bodies or means of expression is
as though they are the "Lower" Self in conjunction with a
"Middle" and "Higher" Self—one way to picture it might be
as a central core, with the Physical or densest vibration in the
center (most solid), and with all of these other systems of
energy, or "bodies," vibrating further out from (and within)
this same core, overlapping, interrelating, and affecting each
other on an energy wave basis.

The Being: *(with mock alarm)* I suppose this means it could really get
crowded in a session with all of these energy systems present!

Astro: *(with a laugh)* To tell you the truth, body integration sessions
with human Beings do deal chiefly with the three base systems, but all the body levels have presence and participate to
a greater or smaller degree, depending on the amount of at-a-
tilt-ness currently held by the Being. While I have hands on a
Being and am merging my energies with theirs for the pur-

pose of reintegrating the three base systems, I also become somewhat of a "life-line" for them to connect their Lower, Middle, and higher Self, since during the process of the work we have pulled various members apart for the purpose of working with them and eventually re-relating them in a more integrated form. After the experience of working together while being in physical touch, I can later access the total Being through the Mental realm—through the imagination, or "created thought"—without being present in form. In other words, at the moment when something is "up" (to be learned, resolved, or unfolded), and it reaches the conscious Being through the thought that enters their head, I can offer my vibration as an amperage booster for the Being to help bring that aspect (the thing that is "up") into integration amongst the Being's members.

Being: *(excitedly sensing the new possibilities in store for Itself because Its members have aligned)* So, when the systems begin to come into alignment and balance and all three begin to function in the moment, how are things different?

Astro: *(beaming)* When all the systems come "on line," the Being experiences harmony, through a realignment of personal worth. And life in harmony with creation, knows what is real: true reality. In other words, when God or all-of-totality, connects through the Heart and is supported through Mind, you experience Integration.

In terms of the individual members, the Mental body expresses this harmony through **Integrity**, by seeing that words and actions match, and seeing that our "standards" work— that is, we stand in our truth. The Mind gets bad press because of its incessant internal chattering. However, when the Mind expresses full Integrity, this chatter shifts to one of one hundred percent harmonious support as it gives up trying to do the work of one or both of the other chairpersons. The Emotional member contributes harmony through **Intimacy**, allowed by feelings of safety and freedom. Thus, when **Integrity** aligns with **Intimacy**, **Integration** results—Being in flow and full Self-expression, and the Physical member expresses the harmony of well-being. **Integration** is the goal, both in the inner domain and in the outer world of relationships. Integration results in feeling connected, within ourselves and to All That Is.

So, when you back your "Self" no matter what, you open the space for others to support you and to see you as a Living Example of individual Magnificence.

Being: *(making the connection to one of Astro's oft-repeated phrases)* That Incredible, Magnificent, Priceless Gift you often mention?

Astro: *(thrilled)* Exactly. **Truth** is "getting" your Priceless-ness and knowing that no one is standing behind you to establish your value for you, because it is a given. In other words, we, the universe, count on You to do You. And I emphasize the word "Priceless" because, in fact, dollars tend to de-value people, since in reality we are all "Priceless Gifts" as human Beings. The notion of dollars related to value is a complete misnomer in terms of true reality. If we have too few dollars, anyone caught up in typical reality will tend to view us as less valuable, and if we have more dollars than we need, we appear as though our value is greater than others'. If you believe this illusion, then if you have excess dollars, you might begin to think that you are better than others and subconsciously begin to limit others or show force over others, or vice versa.

As awareness shifts on the planet, and Connected-ness becomes the standard in conscious-ness, Value will cease to be determined in terms of having or not having an item, but rather in terms of the Quality of Presence or Interaction with said item, for it is the quality of presence or interaction that produces fulfillment.

Also, the gift of our Magnificence doesn't mean we don't all fall short, mess up, or act silly; what it means is that we all have the healing factors of forgiveness and laughter as we learn to edit out all items that keep us from going forward in life and to "vision in" the values and items that nurture us and support us fully and unconditionally, as well as to ease the seriousness with which we view our life and the lessons in it. Interwoven into the fibers of these two healing factors that grow with use is LOVE, that eternal knowing-ness that dissolves the separation caused by dis-connected notions of "I'm right; you're wrong." Love doesn't point its finger at anyone. It fosters wholeness. Again, it's as though we are a beautiful, glowing laser beam of colored thread, lovely in our own right and yet more awesome as we are interwoven in the tapestry of life with other glowing threads.

Amethyst Crystal: *(shimmering brilliantly and waving its purple vibration in earnest)* Are you saying that forgiveness and laughter are our healing factors that enable us to experience our Magnificence?

Astro: *(thoroughly enjoying the Mental member's rediscovered light-ness)* Yes, and this Magnificence we experience shows up in a loving way.

Amethyst Crystal: *(intensely pursuing its train of thought)* Kind of like a natural talent?

Astro: *(noting also the sincere level of interest)* Not exactly. These factors are the means that enable us to get out from under our own overwhelming situations or mishaps. These healing factors are a *given,* whether in use or not, a lot like natural *gifts,* whereas natural *talents* are inclinations we have that we pursue and develop. Our natural gifts are things we do *so* easily, in fact, that we don't see them as anything special. For example, some people can nurture children with no effort, or perhaps someone shares mercy as effortlessly as they breathe. These are natural *gifts*—which are our "givens" that we can be grateful for—whereas *talents* relate to items we learn easily and have an enthusiastic interest in developing. Therefore, our natural gifts are about Being-ness, about All That Is as expressed through us. All natural gifts benefit humanity across the board—and some of these values also show up as talents, because they can be *developed* through choice and interest.

All of us, while in form, seem to find ourselves in different situations and faced with different items that we consider important to us. Some folks, through these gifts, have the ability to let go, grow, or change belief systems and shift priorities, more easily than others.

Natural talents, on the other hand, are about "doing-ness"— what we're inclined toward to learn more about and get good at. A talent, then, is that which is developed, and which may or may not be of interest to everyone.

(making a shift to a new angle) While we're on the subject of gifts, it is only while experiencing Integration that we can

truly *give* to others, as well as truly *receive* from others, since you can't give or receive from another what you haven't yet fully given to yourself, such as forgiveness, love, understanding, compassion, and so on.

The flow has to operate both ways, however, because you will find Mentally-based Beings who are great givers, because they like to "do" their love by making it visible, but many find it hard to receive, because when receiving they are out of control. If a Being is always the giver, which equals "always being in charge of when and how much is given," then who is there to receive? Thus, the full experience of giving gets short-circuited.

Emotionally-based Beings also like to give, but tend to do so because they feel like it, and their ability to receive is determined by their sense of their own worthiness and wanting to share that experience of value with another. And yet, even then, if they feel like they are not being appreciated or are being used, they will pull back in a flash and withhold themselves as well as their thoughts and material items.

There's a poem I've run across that really says it for me:

> "Giving's receiving,
> Receiving is giving;
> That's truly the joy
> That lies behind living.
> So give something each day,
> And you'll find that it's true,
> All the gifts of the Heart
> Will be given to you."

(as Astro pauses for emphasis, it sees the Being wiping a tear off its energy field, and knows the gist of the poem has been received)

Astro: *(again warming to its subject)* In fact, in the natural flow of abundant energy, it is designed for us to get back not only what we have given, but rather to get back more—encouraging us to give more, and so on, and so on, and so on.

(Astro, pausing long enough to see four sets of awarenesses once again in a state of awe and overwhelm at the magnitude of Astro's sharing, moves to conclude the day's input)

To pull the idea full circle and sum up everything we've covered, our one-ness is our most basic relationship, the relationship with the "Self," our own nature. We work on a relationship through interactions with ourselves and others. Through these experiences, we discover that although we humans are all doing the same program—we are born, live our lives, and die—each of us is also uniquely different. Going back to the image of the spokes of a wheel, all of the spokes lead to the hub in the center and are equidistant from each other for balance and strength, and yet each is at a slightly different vantage point—no better, no worse—just a different perception. Given the fact that we all have different lessons to learn, how we interpret those lessons determines whether our position on the wheel (our perception) frees our thinking, feeling, or actions, or whether it immobilizes us, Mentally, Emotionally, or Physically.

(now bringing the focus back to the "Being") When looking outside of the "Self" to determine your place in the world and passing judgment on what you see, you set in motion the

notion of being separate from that particular situation or person (or another part of the whole), and you begin to vibrate less fully as a representative of the one-ness we all are.

However, when you show up in your space of knowing-ness that remembers we are all one, you tend to include all of life and become a Living Example—"walking your talk" by having your words and actions match—and this expression of wholeness encourages others to do likewise. At the risk of repeating myself, when you do YOU and pay attention to your world and your life story, others are supported to do the same for themselves.

That's why the words "making a difference" form such a conscious phrase, because each of our individual universes dictates how the world looks to us. That's why you cannot make anyone look at the world the way YOU want them to, by manipulation, victimization, or bullying. You are a universe unto yourself, one that is beautifully synchronized with the universe around you, when your words and actions match. When you know you are full and complete in yourself, attachment disappears. No loss of appreciation, but rather an enhanced experience of the Gift it is to be in form with other human Beings—in short, Gratitude. That goes back to having a fertile field of compassion in which to place one's under-standing, a place connecting Acceptance to Gratitude.

Ultimately, being a "Living Example of connected-ness" means backing and honoring your true Self, even when there's no receptivity from co-workers or loved ones. When you start to move into this place of wholeness, there are bound to be obstacles to overcome as your full Magnificence starts to shine. That's why honoring an individual's position, as themselves, as they see it, enables you to remain "whole" and go forward in your own life.

So, bottom line, how you view and hold your "Self," and therefore how you present your "Self," affects how others respond to you as well as how they look or seem to you. Your presentation of "Self" can even affect how they hold or perceive themselves!

As mentioned before, the key to living this life and seemingly a most difficult feat for most human Beings to accomplish is to let your Self "have" the experience you are having, *when you are having it*—and, once completed, to have the freedom to move on to the next item up for you. Some of the lessons may look repetitive, and yet we are not the same person each time that lesson comes up. And, just like stepping into a moving stream, we can continue to flow with what comes up, and grow, or we can work very hard to appear to maintain sameness.

However, once again, by not resisting or denying the moment of awareness, and by being able to sit in embarrassment or any non-agreement, you open the door to have the experience at hand. And, by backing the "Self" exactly where you are at, by stating your truth about it, even when you fall short of the mark or desired goal, you support your "Self," making room for others to do so as well. This action gives you the "space" to complete the communication or lesson at hand. It also releases you from carrying around, in your conscious-ness and conversation, other people, unresolved issues, and unex-pressed feelings, creating a new position from which to view the next Eternal Moment of Now.

And the other key is that *the Being cannot be harmed!* It can be curtailed, imprisoned, discounted, or unsupported—but it cannot be harmed, except by ourselves, for we are the only person who truly knows how life looks to us, and what has motivated our actions.

So, once again, in our Incredible Magnificence, we don't have to do, be, or have anything to be of value. We can let go of all shoulds, coulds, woulds, oughts, and similar words, because none of those have anything to do with the Priceless nature that we all are. In the words of Sathya Sai Baba, "Birth as a human being is considered a rare gift."

(with heart-felt emotion) So, from my viiewing place, it is indeed a privilege and a pleasure to spend time with another Being. For how we relate in life with other Beings is directly related to how we relate within ourselves to and between our own Mental, Emotional, and Physical bodies. When we experience the magic of our own oneness, all others and the world we are a part of become magical in our view.

(Astro, having said about all it could think of, lays back into the grass, feeling quite spent and fulfilled at the same time)

(The Being and Its members gaze intently and fondly at each other while they all wonder how much of what they have just learned and experienced will stay with them, realizing it will take four to six weeks to prove out before these possible new belief items get set in motion as new habit energies.

(But at this particular moment, the Being and each of its members remain silently caught up in their own viewing points of possible shifts in perceptions, and at the awesomeness of the vast, infinite possibilites that life has to offer.)

. . . And before you leave the marketplace, see that no one has gone his way with empty hands. For the Master Spirit of the Earth shall not sleep peacefully upon the wind till the needs of the least of you are satisfied.

—Kahlil Gibran, *The Prophet*

All must lead, to know what it is to fully integrate knowingness of understanding.

—Marlo Morgan, *Mutant Message Down Under*

A wise man does not choose to change the destiny of another.

—Anonymous

For the world to work for any one of us, it must work for everyone.

—Werner Erhard

If you bury yourself in any one experience,
you'll prevent yourself from having new ones.

—Yanni

♡ EPILOGUE ♡

THE SWAMP
NEXT TO THE MOUNTAIN

(After a few moments, Astro stands by as the Being and her
members ponder the day's insights in deep appreciation and
wonder.)

Astro: *(gently breaking the silence)* If no one has any additional questions, I believe congratulatory hugs are in order for each and every one of you, individually and together. For you have been very busy here today and will experience the results of your efforts, I believe, for years to come. I, for one, am very proud of you all.

(As the Being again hugs the new visions of Its three densest
bodies, through which It expresses Itself in daily life, Astro
hands the Being some papers to be handed personally to
Foot, before the Symposium ends. Absent-mindedly, the pa-
pers are accepted by the energy field of the Being, who does
not notice the tears of joy on Astro's face.)

(Having the desire to hug everyone at the Symposium, the
Being and Its new members start to get up and return to the
conference.)

242

(Looking around and noticing that Astro is nowhere in sight, they each "assume," as they had been hugging so passionately, that the Astral Body Therapist had left them alone to go on ahead of them. As the group crosses the street, returning to the building where the symposium is being held, the Being ponders how strange yet vaguely familiar Its three densest bodies seem now, in these, their more powerful visions. Knowing the strength of habit energy, It realizes that Its experiences with Deer, Jaguar, and Wizard will stay with the Being for a long time. The Being knows that, had those initial visions not come forward, It would not have had the opportunity to become as completely aware of Its full potential.)

(The Being feels a glow of accomplishment and awareness within, along with a surge of energy that feels greater than any form could hold, and It wonders whether there will be any Physical discomfort when Itself and all Its members realign within the Physical skin suit. . . . and somehow It knows that the opposite would be true.)

(At that moment, the Being's thoughts are distracted by the sight before them. As they enter the auditorium, all of the individual Body Parts in the huge room are glowing and applauding tremendously—yet not a light is on, except on the stage, where Foot waits patiently. It occurs to the Being that while Itself and Its members have been outside in the park, releasing, growing, and realigning, some pretty wonderful things have been going on in the symposium, too.)

(Finally, the room falls silent, and Foot, this year's chair of ceremonies, begins to speak:)

Foot: *(on the verge of tears of wonderment)* What a day we have had! To say it has far exceeded my personal expectations is putting it mildly. I want to thank each and every one of you participants for coming today and for being willing to accept all the last-minute changes in the program. I had wanted to thank the lone Being and Astro, the Astral Body Therapist, again, by asking them to join me on stage, only I've just learned that neither of the two are in the room, and Astro wasn't even on the official program for today. In fact, no one on the organizing committee seems to know Astro at all. So, on behalf of all of our speakers . . .

The Being: *(having worked Itself all the way to the front of the room)* Excuse me . . . excuse me. I have some papers here that Astro asked me to give to you to share at the end of the day. And even though we have no clue as to Astro's origins, I would feel incomplete if these words went unspoken.

Foot: *(beaming at the Being)* Thank you, thank you, Being. Please come up here on stage so we can all acknowledge you . . .

(a standing ovation rocks the rafters)

. . . and, since you seem to have materialized this amazing speaker, I'd like you to share its notes with us. But first, I want to thank you for your contributions in furthering the experience we all shared earlier today. Next year, I do hope more Beings will come to participate with their members, as well as another fantastic turnout of individual Body Parts.

(the thunderous applause reaches deafening proportions)

(meanwhile, the Being, as full awareness, can clearly tell that Its sharing had made a difference in the quality of experience for these Body Parts, as well as for Itself)

The Being: *(overcome, stuttering)* I . . . I am so moved, . . . I . . . I can hardly speak. Actually, I don't even know what is in these notes I carry, but I know Astro wanted you all to hear this. I see it's a story entitled "The Swamp Next to the Mountain."

(taking a moment to compose Itself)

You see, it says, there's this swamp next to a mountain. And in the swamp, it is deep, dark, dank, and dismal, and the weather is always foggy, eerie, mucky, and dreary.

(a few snickers break out at the poetic descriptions)

Now . . . there are some people in the swamp who don't want to get out; they are held back by pride, anger, drink, or a sense of being owed something. And you want to avoid these people, because all they can do is pull you under while any such attitudes of separateness prevail.

And then there are some other people in the swamp who want to get out of it. They are ready to try out a new awareness, but it takes a really strongly-centered person to assist each one in that process, because habit energy is in full operation, and whoever is assisting with bringing in the new awareness has to be careful that they don't get pulled down into the swamp water accidentally.

And then there are the rest of us, up on dry land and heading up the mountain. So, one of us starts moving up the mountain—and almost instantly, the heaviness of the swamp area is replaced with tiny pockets of sunshine working its way through the dense fog, and we find ourselves at a place to rest, where a little blue sky and fresh air can be seen and felt. So, we call down to a friend, "Hey, down there—you think it's great just being on land—but let me say, there's much more to experience up here. Why don't you come on up and see?"

And as that friend clears off a few more of the cobwebs from its Self, full of old notions and misperceptions, it treks on up to where you are pleasantly sitting on a rock. Immediately, your friend becomes aware of how much lighter it feels and just how beautiful even a sliver of blue sky is—and how this height enables one to see even further than one's immediate domain.

However, you look up and say, "Well, this is nice, but wow!—look at that ledge up there. Let's go check it out."

Then your friend says, "Sounds great, but I like it here. You go on ahead."

And off you go.

By the time you get to the ledge you had spotted, the clouds are now fluffy white in a clearing sky, and you can see far and wide, over hill and dale, across a land of beautiful meadows of lovely wild flowers, trees, and streams—and Self-respect is starting to replace Self-doubt and recriminations. You yell down, "I know you like it down there, but really—this is such a sight to see! I had no idea such awesome diversity existed on this planet—you really must see it!"

And so, having rested for a while, your friend decides to expand its view of the world by beginning to support itself more fully, and then to make the journey up to the ledge where you are standing. Upon arriving, the friend is so dazed by the breath-taking views that its curiosity is thoroughly aroused, and, before you even realize it, your friend is by-passing you to even greater heights, where oceans and whole forests and even dreams are visible . . . .

(moving into the wonder of being in form and knowing that all of creation is one awareness)

And so we are all constantly leap-frogging each other, bringing new and wondrous feelings and thoughts to our relationships and to ourselves—until we finally get to the top of the mountain, with its 360 degree view. And, for that one, brief, Eternal Moment of Now, you experience who you really are—an Incredible, Magnificent, Priceless Gift, what life is all about, and your personal part in the gigantic puzzle of dualities—as whole and complete through Acceptance and Gratitude. . . .

—and then you happen to look over, and there's a *bigger* swamp next to a *bigger* mountain. . .

(the Being pauses at length to let the implications of this information seep in)

(continuing to read aloud) For you see, every one of us has sat on mountaintops. Whether we understand why we are in a swamp, or why someone we care about is in one, has nothing to do with our natural Magnificence, nor alters our stature as a Priceless Gift, which IS, just by our being here. The whole question is whether or not you choose to continue to see yourself as separate or as an intricate part of the whole. The Being in the swamp believes itself to be separate—so Hope is not an option. This is why our court system does not include the Emotional member—for those on trial really believe they are not connected to the whole and must be dealt with as such. It simply isn't possible to approach someone with the notion

of being *related* when they do not entertain the idea for themselves. Only those who have bridged the gap between their perceived experience and their protective thinking can be assisted out of the swamp. Even then, habit-energy can pull them down again into the swamp, if they are not as yet self-generating.

However, for the world to work fully for any one of us, it must work for everyone. And furthermore, all of life deserves a happy ending. Therefore, we, as Beings, have reached that critical point in our human development where ignorance is no longer an option, for we remember that we have sat on mountaintops. We now know, in our heart of hearts, that the choice is ours—whether to give up our notion of being individual, lone ducks in the pond and to embrace our totality, as reflected in peace, happiness, and fulfillment—or not. I personally believe that we, on this planet, have reached that point where enough Beings are ready to claim their Magnificence. And when enough vibration and energy shifts its focus, the rest is destined to follow or dissolve itself.

Sadly though, and ironically, we are going to miss these days of struggle and upset. For as awful as life has seemed to be at times, it is this particular time on the planet Earth of which we will someday say, "We were there when perception shifted."

We won't have to read about it in the history books. We *are* the Living Examples of this change from a mode of determining the Self through outside forces to one of looking within and finding home. As wondrous as all of the technological advances we have witnessed so far, they dim considerably when placed in the light of an expanded awareness of totality.

So, my message is to take stock and see where you are. If abundant flow is not a natural occurrence in your life, somewhere the notion of isolation is in operation. You really are the chooser, and the choices are getting clearer daily. We have known the answer for some time. It is repeated over and over in many books from many voices and lands. We even speak it to each other . . . but no one can make the actual shift for us: that is the critical point we all face. And, like the swamp next to the mountain, it matters not whether you take the plunge today—or ever—to expand your awareness, because only You signed up to be You.

It is for the rest of us to honor your choice of action—*or lack thereof*—and accept that as your truth. You have to go within to find your own answers. By doing so, the answers will always filter through the three dense systems—the Physical, Emotional, and Mental. So I repeat, only You have the answers for You, and it isn't good, bad, or indifferent if someone stays in the swamp or is actively moving up the mountain. The important factor is having enough faith and giving unconditional support to *all Beings* so they truly can choose to remain where they are or to grow into the light and sound of wholeness. As we really are all one, our respect demands that we give the same gift to others that we have received. For, after all our moaning, groaning, weeping, wailing, and difficult unfoldments, the joy came when *we* realized our *Self*. So let's not spoil it for other portions of the whole. After all, when telling a joke, we like to be the one who delivers the punch line.

In the meantime, we are left with the really big challenge of being a Living Example of who and what we all are. Believe me, it's harder than you think to get out of someone's way and let them discover their truth for themselves. Many Beings erroneously think the game is over at this point, because the struggle is gone, but I say the original game is just beginning—the game of knowing our oneness and yet operating in what appears to be separate units. Such an opportunity has not been on the planet Earth since the vibrations of Mystical, Magical Awarenesses were plentiful. But that story is for another book. . . .

(the Being looks over at the Unicorn, Amethyst Crystal, and Gabriella, wondering about the reference to Mystical, Magical Awarenesses and what that energy might have to do with third-dimensional living, and hopes they will get the chance to find out soon . . .)

*   *   *

. . . and this is the wonder

that's keeping the stars apart—

i carry your heart

(i carry it in my heart)

—e.e. cummings*

*Excerpted from "i carry your heart with me" by E.E. Cummings.

ABOUT THE AUTHOR

Jeanie Lemaire, a humanist and body therapist, travels throughout the United States and Canada, providing the safe space for people to realize their Magnificence through Physical, Mental, and Emotional body integration. She is available for lectures and a certain number of private body therapy sessions. In honor of the processes within this book, the author has chosen not to have her photo on the back cover. Like Gibran's Prophet, she is a wanderer and an observer of the environment in which we all live our lives. She recognizes that she is but a piece of this puzzle we call the universe, one individual perception of life in process, no greater or less than any other aspect. She is lovingly dedicated to supporting individual Magnificence as it is expressed around the globe.

Should you wish to contact her or share your experience of personal awareness with her, please direct your communication to the publisher.

ABOUT THE EDITOR

Corinn Codye's multiple talents have a common thread: the ability to creatively manifest and enhance "flow and connection"—whether it be in practicing and guiding students in t'ai chi, designing and writing educational materials, authoring children's literature, or serving as a "creative media translator" (as in this work) for authors and publishers. Her deepest dedication is to universal Truth, to the beneficial inner growth of all Beings, that all may happily realize their true nature and fully experience truth, love, beauty, and goodness. She may be contacted at Balancing Arts, P.O. Box 3864, La Habra, CA 90632-3864, telephone (310) 694-1229.

A sequel originated by Jeanie Lemaire and co-written with Corinn Codye,

BEING

* Human & Divine Through Mystical, Magical Awareness *

is in progress and scheduled for publication in 1996. To contact the author or to receive an announcement of its publication, please write or call:

Balancing Arts
P.O. Box 3864
La Habra, CA 90632-3864
310-694-1229